CONTAINER AND RAISED BED GARDENING
FOR BEGINNERS AND BEYOND

A Guide to Growing your own
Vegetables, Herbs, Fruit and Cut Flowers

WENDY SILVEIRA

ISBN: 978-0-578-77820-4

Cover Image:
Photography: All photos via Adobe Stock, except Wendy Silveira, pages 126 through 133.
Illustrations, pages 19, 20, 21: Gemini.
All floral arrangements come from the author's garden.

Affiliate Disclosure:
This book has affiliate links. If you buy using my links, at no additional cost to you,
I get a small commission so I can write even more great books!

just for you!

To receive your free e-book
Getting the most out of tomatoes,
as well as my signature recipe for
Garlic Roasted Tomato Soup, sign up at
wendysgardenstore.com/free-gift/

Dedication

This book is dedicated to my family who blessed me with wonderful gardening genes: My Gran, a founder member of the first horticultural society in South Africa, Uncle Charles who introduced me to roses, and my beloved Mom, Miss Thellie, who spent so many happy hours in the garden with me. And last, but certainly not least, my husband who has been my north star, both in the garden and in life, and without whom this book would not have been written. I love you all.

Table of Contents

Introduction

Have you ever wandered through a farmer's market and marveled at the array of fresh vegetables, herbs, fruit and cut flowers?

Did you find yourself dreaming of being able to grow your own? Perhaps you were brought down to earth when you remembered your limited space, or even recalled your not-so-green thumb which has let you down countless times!

Well, help is at hand: Drawing upon a lifetime of gardening experience, come with me as we journey down the garden path to a bounty of vegetables, herbs, fruit and cut flowers. By using a highly successful method – growing *above-ground* in **containers** or **raised beds**, or a combination of both, I will show you how to become a successful urban gardener in whatever space is available to you.

In just a short time you can be harvesting your own garden-fresh, organic produce throughout the year; the sooner you plant, the sooner you reap the benefits!

Each chapter presents clear and concise information which will enable you to reach your gardening goals, without intimidating even the beginner gardener. Useful tips along the way provide every-day, common sense solutions to gardening problems.

Coupled with all the information you need to grow a wide variety of vegetables, herbs, fruit and cut flowers, are my tried and tested signature recipes: Savor the aroma of a pot of Spaghetti Bolognese sauce simmering on the stove, enhanced by Italian herbs grown in your own garden.

Join me as we decode gardening basics, learn what's involved in sowing seed, understand the process of planning your garden, and explore quick-reference growing guides for edibles and cut flowers; finally enjoy the fruits of your labors from *your* garden to *your* table.

Biography

Born and raised in South Africa, I have been an avid gardener and amateur horticulturalist my whole life.

My life-long passion for gardening took root many years ago when, as a child, I came across my first seed catalog while visiting family. A dull, Sunday afternoon was instantly transformed, and so began my love affair with all-things plants. From edibles to ornamentals, I have always been fascinated by their infinite variety and the joy that gardening brings.

Having grown up with many wonderful gardening books, I found the lack of plant varieties in South Africa frustrating. This led me to spearhead a campaign to import Chinese Tree peonies. This was the first time they had ever been available, and it took the gardening community by storm!

This developed into a successful mail-order business, which resulted in my contributing to a leading South African gardening magazine.

My love of English cottage garden plants led me to import and propagate many plant varieties, which were also new to South Africa. Fellow gardeners shared my joy in being able to grow these plants at last, and it led to my giving many lectures at garden clubs.

My horticultural journey took a detour when I moved to the United States. Not surprisingly, the peony mail order business morphed into a successful internet company.

Whether growing vegetables or herbs or harvesting fruit, the magic of growing plants continues to thrill me. Seeing plants that you have nurtured grow from seed or seedling to reach their full potential of fruit and flowers is like therapy in a gardening glove!

The allure of picking flowers from my garden is something that I never tire of. From simple cosmos to spectacular lilies, bringing the magic of the garden into the house brings me enormous pleasure. I hope that you will try a few of the cut flowers described in the growing guides.

As an avid cook and baker, there has been a natural spillover from garden to table. Being able to pick a fresh lemon and transform it into a Lemon Madeira loaf is something I treasure. Picking herbs and elevating a Spaghetti Bolognese sauce also never grows old. This prompted me to include a list of tried and tested recipes, using some of the harvest from the garden. I hope you enjoy the recipes as much as we do.

Having taught English for many years, sharing knowledge is an integral part of who I am. Combined with a lifetime of garden experience, the next logical step was to share my gardening knowledge in a book.

If you are a beginner gardener, or somewhere beyond, I hope you able to put this knowledge to good use and find the same joy in gardening as I have.

Chapter 1

Take Your Garden to a Higher Level

Above-Ground Gardening in Containers, Raised Beds and Vertical Gardens

---

"Gardening is learning, learning, learning.
That's the fun of them. You're always learning"
– Helen Mirren

In chapter one we will explore the world of above-ground gardening: gardening in containers, raised beds, and even vertical gardening.

The essence of this approach is that every square inch is used to the max!

This enables the urban gardener to leverage whatever gardening real estate is available to them.

In-ground gardening with wide rows between plants

Before we can explore what makes *above-ground gardening* so successful, it's important to understand how this method differs from its traditional 'cousin' - *in-ground gardening*.

In-ground gardening can be back-breaking, slow and costly. It's also *not urban-friendly*, as it takes a lot of space; vegetables are grown *in rows* with 2-feet between rows to allow access.

This traditional gardening method often has disappointing results. This is because many garden soils are depleted in nutrients; they simply don't have the ability to produce a good harvest. Small wonder the beginner gardener blames their lack of success on their 'not-so-green-thumb'!

On the other hand, **above-ground gardening** is often a sure way to jump-start your urban garden and get quick, bountiful results.

The secret lies in the *quality of the soil mix*; instead of trying to improve the soil quality in large garden beds, all the effort is concentrated in a *defined, smaller area*.

As my Gran used to say, "How can the plants not grow!" Good quality soil mix ensures that you can plant your crops closer together; a boon for the urban gardener with limited gardening space.

There are three types of above-ground gardening: **containers**, **raised beds** and **vertical gardening.**

Let's explore each of these options:

The quality of the soil mix allows for closer planting in above-ground gardening

1. Containers

If you have limited garden space available to you, this is probably your best bet. From deck to balcony, containers enable one to raise a good quantity of vegetables, herbs and flowers.

And don't let that stop you growing fruit either. The key is to select a dwarf variety – more on that later in the growing guides in chapter 6.

Vegetables, herbs and flowers flourishing in containers

So many choices! You only have to stroll through a garden center to appreciate that containers are big business today. The choice includes wood, traditional terra cotta, ceramic, plastic, etc. There are even environmentally-friendly fiber pots; they are good for the planet and promote healthier root growth.

It's not only the choice of gardening containers that's overwhelming, but there is also a mind-blowing range of gardening products available. To make life easier for you, I've created a gardening collection of everything you could possibly need, from containers and raised beds kits, to gardening gifts, and many things in between. All of these items are available at **wendysgardenstore.com/store**.

As the chapters unfold and you continue on your gardening journey, you will come across many products that will make you a more successful gardener. To save you time searching for them, I've put these products in easily accessible categories in my shop; I've taken the time to do this, so you don't have to!

Size does matter! As a general rule of thumb, bigger is better; bigger containers allow the roots of large plants to reach their full potential.

If there's space, you can even fill the container with other compatible plants. But that still doesn't answer the beginner gardener's question of which pot for which plant. We will explore this in more detail in chapter 5.

Kale growing in a pot interplanted with marigolds

Location, location, location! To succeed with containers, pick the right spot. Most edibles – fruit, vegetables and herbs – thrive in full sun; most require at least six hours of sun a day. Ornamentals like cut flowers also tend to require a sunny location. Containers allow you the luxury of being able to move them and take advantage of micro-climate spots in your garden year-round.

So, your garden tends to be shady! Make your shady areas work for you; I move my container of mint to a shaded spot in summer, which makes for a 'happy' herb that I don't have to water so often. When getting too much sun, leafy vegetables like lettuce are inclined to *bolt* and form seed before their time. Growing them in a shady spot will help delay this from happening.

And let's not forget the potted Lemon tree which can't tolerate frost. Put this container on a wheeled planter caddy and you can move it indoors during the colder months.

It's not dirt when it's in a pot! Don't be tempted to fill your containers with soil from your garden. Choose the best potting soil that your budget will allow. The old adage holds true: The more you put into it, the more you'll take out of it. More to come on this in chapter 3.

Plants get thirsty! Containers dry out quicker than raised beds. As the plant grows, so it will require more watering. If your lifestyle does not allow you to water regularly, then consider installing a drip irrigation system that takes the work out watering. If your budget permits, a timer system is even better.

Be water-wise and use *self-watering containers* that store water in the base, but don't forget to top up the reservoir – these containers prevent plants from drying out quickly.

A mulch of pine bark creates a layer of protection

Mulching is another great way of cutting back on the chore of watering by placing a layer of material to conserve moisture around the base of the plant, and feed at the same time. More on this in chapter 3.

Feed me! Because nutrients will be flushed out of the container, you will want to feed your container plants with fertilizer during the season.

Stop the press! The biggest reason why people fail to grow plants successfully in containers is that they don't provide adequate *drainage*. Before planting, check the underside of the pot; there should be at least one drainage hole, and more in larger containers. Don't hesitate to make a couple of extra holes. You can also use 'pot risers' to slightly elevate your pots. Do what you have to do to ensure that your container drains well and that your plants don't suffer from *'wet feet'*; for the bakers out there, the horticultural equivalent of Mary Berry's dreaded 'soggy bottom'!

In chapter three we will decode soil basics and explore all these concepts in more detail.

2. Raised Beds

You may be asking yourself what is the difference between a container and a raised bed. In a nutshell, containers have a base, raised beds don't. A raised bed is essentially a frame placed directly on the ground. It can even be situated on hard standing areas like patios and paving; just make sure that they can accommodate the considerable weight of a filled raised bed.

Wooden raised bed with vegetables and flowers

Raised beds are often *square*, generally 4' x 4', or *rectangular* - 8' x 4' is a popular choice.

If space permits, and you have a level area with at **six hours of sun**, and you have the budget, then a raised bed of whatever shape is a great option.

Metal raised beds offer another choice

What are raised beds made from? They can be made of seasoned wood, recycled plastic, galvanized steel, cinder blocks, or even brick. When making the choice, consider where you live: You want your beds to be durable. If you live in a humid, rainy area, then wooden beds may not be the best option for you.

So, what's it going to cost? It is important to realize that there is some *initial outlay* involved - the cost of the raised bed itself, as well as the soil mix to fill it. While the initial investment may seem on the high side, future maintenance is minimal.

There are ways of reducing the expense:

- The do-it-yourself (DIY) enthusiast can easily build a raised bed. (Chapter 2 provides detailed instructions on how to do this.)

- While not the best practice, you can cut costs on the soil mix – more on that in chapter 3.

"Help! I'm useless with a hammer." Perhaps you have a friend or relative who can build it for you. If not, fortunately, raised beds are conveniently available in **kit form** in a variety of shapes, sizes, and materials.

If you've chosen to go with a rectangular raised bed, then you need to decide what **size** suits you:

- Don't be tempted to go too wide: Restrict the **width** to 4 feet; you need access to the middle of the bed from both sides. You don't want to have to climb into the bed to reach plants; that would compact the soil and you want to avoid this at all costs.

- If you are going to locate the raised bed *against an obstacle* like a fence or building, then restrict the width to 2 feet. **The golden rule is to be able to access all parts of the raised bed as comfortably as possible.**

- The ideal **length** of the bed is 8 feet: Any longer than that may result in unnecessary walking. If your raised bed is located along a fence, this wouldn't apply.

Which way should my bed face? Your raised bed should be orientated from **north to south**. This will enable the entire bed to *receive sunlight throughout the day.*

> **Always orientate your raised beds from north to south, not west to east.**

If you erect a permanent *trellis structure*, then this should be located at the **northern end** of the bed. Otherwise, the plants on the structure will shade the rest of the bed. (The opposite will hold true for the southern hemisphere.)

How deep is deep? Whether square or rectangular, the depth of the raised bed is very important. Ideally, you want to have the raised bed as deep as possible to enable the roots to develop fully. A raised bed that is 12" high will accommodate most crops, but there are some crops that will benefit from a higher bed.

Most plants will grow happily in a raised bed of this depth

If bending is an issue, then consider a deeper raised bed. Weigh up the benefits against the cost; the deeper the bed, the more soil mix you will need, and this is where it can become expensive. I will share with you a possible solution for this in chapter 3.

How are you going to water your raised bed? Ideally, you want to install an irrigation system – automated would be nice. Two good irrigation options include a soaker hose system and drip irrigation

. If you can't install irrigation straight away, then at least plan for it in your raised bed design. In the meantime, make sure that there's a convenient water source close at hand.

It's all in the plan!

As you plan where you are going to situate your raised bed, consider that in time to come you may want another. You will want to *allow at least two feet between adjoining beds*; otherwise, you may find that you have to walk sideways between the beds. That could take all the pleasure out of gardening very quickly! If you do have more than one raised bed, then mulch the pathways between them – wood chips and pine needles work well.

Rectangular raised beds separated by gravel pathways

Do I need to remove the grass under my raised bed? The jury's out on this, but if you can, it would certainly be *preferable*. While some folk use 'landscaping fabric' to smother weeds, another option is to line the base of the bed with a thick layer of newspaper or overlapping cardboard. This should kill the grass and any weeds under the raised bed. This material will eventually break down and benefit earthworms, ultimately adding nutrients and organic matter or 'humus' to your soil. If you choose cardboard, then make sure that it extends beyond the raised bed – you don't want grass growing in from outside the raised bed.

Do I need a raised bed liner? If you are locating your raised bed on any hard surface - deck or concrete - then you will need to use a liner to prevent soil from washing out.

Keeping out gophers! Talk to any seasoned gardener and they will tell you horror stories of how they waged war on various critters - not least of which gophers, voles and moles are some of the worst culprits. Since they can decimate your garden overnight, it's wise to take preventative measures before you fill your raised bed. Attaching 'hardware cloth' to the underside of the frame, being careful to overlap it on the edges, will act as an effective barrier. There are instructions in chapter 2 on how to attach this.

Finally, the **elevated raised bed** is a raised bed on legs. This is an absolute boon for the gardener with back or mobility issues.

No bending is priceless

3. Vertical Gardening

Vertical gardening, which involves *growing plants up rather than out,* is nothing new. The beauty of this technique is that it takes very little space, but can pack a big punch - definitely a bonus for the urban gardener with limited gardening real estate.

Tomato "Hundreds and Thousands" is the perfect hanging basket variety

Strictly speaking, a container-grown tomato growing in a tomato cage is considered vertical growing. Other examples include hanging baskets and wall planters which have been around for years. Growing strawberries vertically is also nothing new. Guttering attached to walls creates yet another form of vertical gardening.

What's changed? What *is* new and exciting are the innovative vertical container systems that have become available. They enable the gardener to grow a large number of plants in a very limited space. The vertical hanging wall planter, housing up to 72 plants, is a wonderful way to use a warm wall.

The ingenious **Garden Tower® 2** grows a whopping 50+ plants in just 4 square feet. In addition, it features a central vermicomposting cylinder that feeds the plants.

Vertical containers empower the urban gardener to produce a sizeable crop in a small space; urban gardeners need not be restricted by the confines of a patio or balcony.

Whether or not you choose to grow your garden in containers, raised beds or vertically, remember the mantra *quality vs quantity.* Start small, grow your gardening skills, and above all enjoy the gardening journey!

Chapter 2

If I Had a Hammer!

How to Construct a Raised Bed

Flowers grow in inches, but are destroyed by feet.
~ Gardening Saying

As I mentioned in chapter 1, raised beds are readily available in kit form. However, the convenience of a raised bed kit does come at a cost.

This chapter explains how to make a raised bed using fairly basic carpentry tools, without breaking the bank.

Follow these step-by-step directions to build an **8-by-4-foot raised bed** with a depth of 12 inches using pre-cut untreated wood – Cedar and Redwood are extremely water and rot-resistant.

1. What materials will I use?

- Two 8-foot-long by 2-inch-wide by 12-inch-high boards (sides)
- Two 4-foot-long by 2-inch-wide by 12-inch-high boards (ends)
- Four 16-inch-long by 4 by 4-inches boards (corner posts*)
- Twenty-four 3 to 3.5-inch deck screws

Extras:

- Three 3- by 5-foot rolls ¼ to ½-inch- mesh 'hardware cloth'
- 3 pieces of **rebar** 10 feet long, but not thicker than ⅜ inch
- Three 12" long 1/2-inch thick PVC pipes
- Floating row cover and earth staples

2. What tools do I need?

- Drill
- 2 Wood-working clamps (preferable)
- Tape measure
- Trowel or spade
- Level
- Gloves
- Staple gun (or hammer and u-staples/tacks)

You can cut corners by not using corner posts, and attach the sides directly to the ends. However, corners provide stability, and are worth the extra time and money.

3. A step-by-step guide to building a raised bed

Step 1: Select a **flat surface**, like a deck, on which to construct the raised bed.

To prevent the wood from splitting, **predrill** three evenly-spaced pilot holes (one size smaller than the screw diameter), about 2 inches in at the end of each of the 4 boards.

Step 2: Position one of the **4-foot boards** on its narrow side edge. Put one of the **16-inch corner posts** *upright* against the board; ensure that is flush (in line) with the end of the board. Use two adjustable wood-working clamps at either end of the upright to prevent it from moving.

Step 3: Then secure the board to the post with three 3 1/2-inch screws.

Remove the woodworking

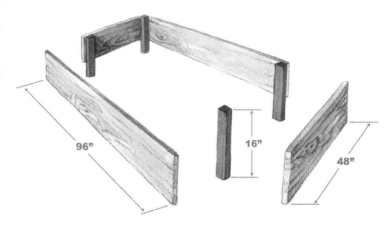

Partially constructed raised bed

clamps and attach another corner post to the other end of this board. Clamp and drill.

Repeat with the other 4-foot board.

Step 4: All that is left to do is to attach the long sides to the two ends. Position the first longboard between the 4-foot bed ends. Ensure the edge is flush with each corner. Clamp and screw.

Remove the clamps and **repeat** with the other 8-foot board.

You've made a raised bed, even if it is upside down

A raised bed is essentially a frame

Step 5: You will need the help of another pair of strong hands to **flip the frame** and move it to the desired position. Using a trowel or spade, dig a 6-inch deep hole where each corner post will be. Move the raised bed with the corner posts over the holes and lower it into position. Use the level to ensure that it is level and stable.

4. Extras

Prevention is better than cure! This is the time to attach your hardware cloth. Use gloves to attach the hardware cloth to the bottom of the raised bed. Attach the material horizontally (not lengthwise) in three overlapping sections. Allow a generous overlap between the strips. Make sure that the cloth is in contact with each of the four sides. Use the staple gun to attach the cloth to the wood. *There should be no gaps.*

> **Be proactive and protect your raised bed against gophers; install hardware cloth before you fill it with soil.**

Additional support: Beds longer than 8' will need to have a **cross-support** in the center. This will prevent the raised bed from bowing out due the pressure of the soil. *Aluminum Flat Bars* are perfect for this job.

Protection against frost or birds: To extend the growing season in colder areas, as well as to protect your crops from birds and pests, you can install a **hoop house;** a framework of hoops covered with row cover (or fleece), or netting. You should do this *before you fill the raised bed.*

For an 8' raised bed you would need to install **three 12" long 1/2-inch thick PVC pipes** vertically inside the raised bed wall on the long side, using galvanized pipe strips. You would do the same on the mirror side.

Raised bed with hoop house

You will need 3 pieces of **rebar** not thicker than 3/8 inch; a length of 10 feet is enough to form a hoop over a 4' wide raised bed. Bend each piece into a half-circle and insert into the pipe. Do the same with its corresponding pipe on the other side of the bed. Repeat with the other two pieces of rebar.

Attach the **floating row cover** to the framework. If your issue is birds rather than frost, you can use chicken wire.

If you are a visual learner like me, you might find it useful to watch an **online video** on YouTube on how to construct a raised bed.

Now it's time to fill your raised bed!

Chapter 3

Decoding Gardening Basics

The Ins and Outs of Gardening

---

*My rule of green thumb for mulch is to double my initial estimate
of bags needed, and add three. Then I'll only be two bags short.*
~Author Unknown

---

*An understanding of gardening basics will em-
power you to make the most of your containers or
raised bed or vertical garden.*

*This chapter gives you all the information that you
will need to successfully grow your own harvest,
from fruit to flowers and everything in between.*

1. The dirt on dirt! Soil care basics

Good soil mix is priceless

Soil is the very lifeblood of the garden. When gardening in containers and raised beds, it is even more important that you **use the very best possible growing medium** to obtain the finest results.

Let's look at **containers** first: Think of the container as a captive audience totally dependent upon you. To make it produce for you, fill your container with a good **potting mix**. This is a balanced mixture of quick-draining, weed-free compost and material – often peat – that retains moisture. My personal preference is Miracle-Gro® Potting Soil. It's consistent, light and airy, and just a great growing medium for all your containers.

What growing medium is best for **raised beds**? They need fluffy, nutrient-rich soil full of organic matter which will enable good root growth that will power the plant. Ideally, use a **pre-bagged medium** specially formulated for raised beds. This medium is slightly heavier than potting mix and more suited to raised beds. I like Miracle-Gro® Performance Organics® Raised Bed Mix. This is guaranteed to get the beginner gardener off to a good, quick start.

So how many bags will I need to fill my raised bed? Use the formula *length x width x depth* to determine the amount of soil you will need.

Let me do the math for you: A raised garden bed that measures 8-feet by 4-feet by 10-inches will need about 27-cubic feet of soil. A bag of Miracle-Gro® Performance Organics® Raised Bed Mix holds 1.3 cubic feet. You will need about 20 bags.

If your raised bed is a different size, then use an online soil calculator to determine how many bags you will need to fill your raised bed. Some have a container option as well.

As I mentioned in chapter one, filling the raised bed is one of the big, once-off outlays; this is why it is prudent to start small. However, if your budget doesn't stretch to using pre-bagged soil mix, then you can *mix your own* custom-planting growing medium:

A standard recipe is:

- 60% topsoil
- 30% compost such as mushroom compost, fine composted wood bark, worm castings, etc.
- 10% potting mix containing peat moss, coir, perlite and/or vermiculite.

Since topsoil forms the bulk of this recipe, it's very important that you get the best possible soil. In the USA you can contact the Cooperative Extension System in your area and see if they can recommend a *reputable* business that sells bulk top soil, and perhaps even compost.

In addition, if your raised bed is deeper than 12 inches, then you don't have to fill the entire bed with growing medium. Instead, you can save money by **'padding'** the lower part of the raised bed (beneath the top 12 inches) with organic material. Line the bottom with branches, leaves, lawn trimmings, pine cones and pine needles, even sliced-up tree stumps. Over time this will break down and decompose, and eventually add nutrients to your growing medium. Cover this organic material with a layer of cardboard, add your raised soil mix, and you have what is known as the *lasagna method* of raised bed gardening

When filling your container or raised bed, remember to stop about **2 inches from the top** – this allows room for a layer of mulch. You will find that some *settling* will occur and the soil may sink slightly. Avoid planting immediately afterwards – give the soil time to settle.

Your soil will need a spa treatment! Amending the growing medium. During its lifetime, the plant, whether container-grown or grown in a raised bed, will rob the soil of its nutrients. If you don't do something about this, the soil will eventually become exhausted, and future crops will become more and more disappointing.

Beans growing in planters with space for mulching

In containers *replace* the entire potting mix at the end of the growing season. On the other hand, **raised beds** can be **rejuvenated** with a product such as *Miracle-Gro® Refresh 1™ Soil Revitalizer*. Spread a layer on top of the soil, fork it into the top layer, plant your transplants, and water. (If you're sowing seed, then wait two weeks.)

Another option is to add a layer of **planting mix** to the raised bed; fork it in lightly; this will aerate and enrich the soil.

Whatever you choose to use, you must *amend* the soil mix in the raised bed, preferably after each crop; think of it as a spa treatment: **Replenish, restore and renew.**

2. After all that, I need a drink! Watering and Irrigation

Effective **watering** is vital to your gardening success. Whether or not you are watering containers or raised beds, there are some golden rules to follow:

- **Water early in the morning**; if your schedule doesn't allow for this, then water in the early evening. Avoid watering in the heat of the day.

- **Avoid wetting the foliage**; direct the water to the roots where it's needed. Otherwise, fungal disease may spread among your plants. To avoid watering the leaves, use a watering wand or lance instead of a watering can.

- **Water deeply** and allow the water to penetrate about **two inches** deep. A strong root system effectively anchors the plant. If you only water the top of the soil, the roots will come to the surface in search of water; a high wind could cause the plant to topple over. The key to effective watering is to give a deep soaking.

- When watering a container, you will need to water until it just starts to run out the bottom

- Plants in containers will need more water than they would in a raised bed. Try to get the whole family on board to help check the plants. It's a great way of involving your children, and fostering a love of gardening in them at an early age. Tomatoes and zucchinis with lots of leafy top-growth will use up the water in the container at an alarming rate.

- Avoid **underwatering** by watering the plant before it wilts and starts to droop

- **Overwatering** can be equally as bad: Perform the fingertip test by digging your finger into the soil about two inches. The soil should feel damp, but not sodden.

Consider investing in an **irrigation system** – it's highly effective and a great help in the garden. There are two systems that are generally used in above-ground gardening:

- **Soaker hoses** allow water to seep out through their entire length

- **Drip irrigation** which allows water to slowly drip directly to the roots of the plant.

Broccoli plants growing in a raised bed with auto drip irrigation system

Both options can be set to run on an **automated timer**, so you don't have to do a thing! Since the water goes directly to the plant's root system, evaporation is greatly reduced and you will *save on your water bill*.

3. What's the scoop on compost?

Compost which is similar to mulch (discussed in the next section), looks a lot like soil. It is *fully decomposed* organic material which acts as a great **soil conditioner**. It may be store-bought or you can make your own.

Bin composters are readily available and are a great way of utilizing kitchen scraps (not meat) and garden trimmings. Choose one that will suit your needs and be easy to use – the tumbler variety is a good option.

Vermicomposting is very much in the news; the process usually involves red wigglers, a type of earthworm, to break down the kitchen scraps and green waste. The decomposed product, known as *worm castings*, is highly prized by gardeners, as it is rich in plant nutrients and beneficial microorganisms. The Garden Tower® 2 mentioned in chapter 1 incorporates a vermicomposter in its design.

In raised beds spread a thick layer of compost – up to 4 inches - on top of the soil *at the end of the growing season*. Cover with a layer of mulch and together they will **amend** the soil.

4. Dress your plants! Mulching

A layer of mulch will protect these young seedlings

So, what is mulch? It includes leaves, straw, compost, wood chips, bark, sawdust, pine needles and grass clippings, etc.

How would I use it? You would apply a *top-dressing* layer about **two-inches thick** on top of the soil around the plant. You want to avoid piling the mulch up against the stem of the plant.

I briefly mentioned some of the **benefits of mulching** in chapter 1:

- It *conserves moisture*; you will not need to water so often
- It *insulates the soil* by keeping it cool in summer and warm in winter
- It *suppresses weeds* by preventing them from germinating.

As if these benefits weren't enough, it will also enrich your soil as it breaks down. **It really is the gardener's friend.**

5. Your plants could use a power boost! Fertilizer

Walk into a garden center and you could be forgiven for feeling overwhelmed by the dizzying array of fertilizer on the shelves. Since it can make a huge difference in your garden, it is really important to understand how it works. So, in this section I will attempt to **demystify fertilizer**.

You might have noticed a series of three numbers on fertilizer products, such as 2-3-2 or 3-1-5 or even 13-0-0. These numbers refer to the **NPK** values, which begs the question, "What is NPK?"

NPK refers to the **macronutrients** that plants need to grow:

- **Nitrogen (N)** promotes leafy growth and keeps plants green. Organic examples include *hoof and horn, blood meal, alfalfa meal, cottonseed* and *fish meal*

- **Phosphorus (P)** encourages strong root growth, and promotes fruiting and flowering. Organic examples include *bone meal, guano* and products marketed as *bulb* or *bloom fertilizer*

- **Potassium (K)** maintains the overall health of the plant. Organic examples include *kelp* and *green sand* which comes from the ocean floor.

In order to thrive, plants also need a slew of **micronutrients**, including *calcium, magnesium, Sulphur, iron* and others. They are used by plants in *trace (small) amounts* and are not usually found in all fertilizer. Be cautious applying micronutrients to your soil. You really need to conduct a *soil test* before you do so. This is a rather specialized horticultural area outside the scope of this book; If you suspect your plant is in distress, take a leaf to your local garden center and ask them for help.

A word of caution: You may think that the higher the fertilizer numbers, the more effective the product. However, when it comes to fertilizer, *more is not necessarily better*!

As a general rule of thumb, use a **balanced** fertilizer in which all three numbers are the same, or close together, for example, **5-5-5 or 2-3-2**. There are some fertilizers specially targeted at specific plants, such as tomatoes, azaleas, citrus, etc. If you are growing these plants, then it makes sense to use a fertilizer specially designed for them.

You will have noticed that I only provided examples of **organic fertilizer** which are *derived from plants and animals*. Apart from the obvious push towards organic fertilizer especially for edibles, there are other reasons why gardeners prefer organic to inorganic or **chemically-derived** fertilizer.

Organic fertilizer *releases* small amounts of nutrients over time – what is known as *slow-release* fertilizer. In contrast, chemical fertilizers feed the plant quickly, but leach out of the soil equally rapidly.

Fertilizer comes in two forms – **granular** (powder), and a fast-acting *water-soluble* **liquid** form.

Stirred not shaken! Liquid fertilizer is a great way to get instant results. It is dissolved in water and is immediately available to the plant's root system. You can apply soluble fertilizer to the base of the plant. For even quicker results, you can do a **foliar feed** directly to the leaves – one of the few times when one deliberately wets the foliage – but do this in the early morning.

Keep the fertilizer away from the stem

Don't kill them with kindness! There's a knack to working with fertilizer:

- **Follow the directions** on the package – don't double up

- Always fertilizer when the soil is **damp**

- Choose a **calm, windless day,** preferably early in the **morning**

- Don't fertilize if rain is the forecast – fertilizer will be lost as nutrients will be leached out of the soil.

Some additional guidelines for applying granular fertilizer are:

- **Sprinkle** the fertilizer *evenly*, but sparingly, on top of the mulch

- Don't let it come in **contact with the leaves** – even organic fertilizers can burn plants

- **Water in well,** and try to avoid wetting the leaves – it's always safer to do this in the morning.

Which fertilizer is preferable and what should I use? They each have their place in the garden:

- I use a granular **'starter'** fertilizer (not lawn starter) at planting time. This fertilizer is specially developed to meet the needs of seedlings or young plants

- About a month later, I follow up with granular all-purpose fertilizer such as 2-3-2

- Continue feeding monthly with a liquid fertilizer throughout the growing season.

I hope this has taken the mystery out of fertilizers and that you feel confident about how to feed your plants.

6. To sow or not to sow! Seed vs transplants

Gardeners are faced with a choice – plant *seed*, or buy *seedlings*, usually sold in packs of six. While the array of seeds may be very tempting, I recommend that you **stick to planting seedlings initially.** Let someone else do the hard work for you and purchase ready-to-plant seedlings, sometimes called 'transplants' or 'starts' from a *reputable* garden center. Before buying your seedlings, have a quick look around. If you see plants with yellow or droopy leaves, or even roots sticking out of the bottom of the container, leave and find another nursery!

Another reason why buying packs of seedlings is a better option for the beginner gardener is that they significantly reduce the amount of time between sowing and harvesting, sometimes by as much as two months. If you live in a colder region, that could be the difference between enjoying the harvest, or losing it to the first early frost!

Never buy more than you can plant within the next week or two. Packs of seedlings should be sold at an optimum stage of their development. If you keep them for too long, the seedlings may become root-bound in their pots – the roots are restricted by the small pots, and go around and around. Not a good start for the plant!

How do you plant out your seedlings? Always water the container or raised bed the day before you transplant. The soil should be *damp*, but not sodden. The best time to plant out your seedlings is *early in the morning*. Avoid doing this in the heat of the day. Handle the transplants carefully; you want to **disturb the roots as little as possible**. Ideally, they should 'pop out' of the 6-pack: Press *one* of the compartments from underneath, and the plant should emerge with its roots intact.

Make a hole the size of the pot and plant the seedling level with the surface. Tomatoes are the exception to this – see the tomato growing guide for more information.

Water the soil around the transplants *gently* immediately after planting. You want to avoid 'drowning' the plant by making the leaves heavy with water.

Planting out a seedling while keeping the roots totally intact

When is sowing seed a better option than transplants? There are a small number of plants which are better grown from seed *directly* in your containers or raised bed, because they don't *transplant* well. These mainly include *root crops* such as carrots, beets, radishes and parsnips, etc.

In chapter 4 I will explain how to sow seed directly. I will also cover starting seed indoors for those gardeners who wish to go this route.

> **Recycle old nylons (tights) by cutting them up into strips - they make great plant ties.**

7. What's at stake? Supporting your plants

Most low growing plants, like parsley and lettuce, do not need any form of support. Taller growing plants, like tomatoes and runner beans, and cut flowers like dahlias, will need help in staying upright; this is where **staking** comes in.

A triangular support structure for beans

Tomato cages are durable and economical

Fortunately, there are easy solutions to achieving this. **Tomato cages** are readily available from garden centers and big-box stores, and come in a variety of sizes. The shorter cages are ideal for peppers, and will even keep a container of gladiolus under control.

Sometimes all that is needed is a stake. Metal plastic-coated stakes come in a variety of lengths and are long-lasting. Bamboo also works well.

Take care when tying up your plant. It should not be too tight; you don't want to strangle it! You can use special planting ties, or follow my tip to recycle old pantyhose. Tomatoes will grow very quickly; aim to stake at regular intervals. When staking up plants, handle the stems very gently; some may be brittle and break easily.

You may wish to erect a permanent trellis in your raised bed. Always position this at the northern end, so as not to shade the rest of the bed. (Reverse this in the southern hemisphere.)

Which plants will need a trellis? Peas (including sweet peas), runner beans, winter squash and cucumbers can all be trained to grow up a trellis.

8. What's the buzz? The role of pollinators

As entertaining as it is to watch bumblebees sucking nectar, or hummingbirds divebombing a flower, these ever-busy **pollinators** are our 'worker bees' in the garden. Along with bees and butterflies, they perform a vital part in pollinating our fruit and vegetables. If you don't have pollinators, you won't get zucchinis, and there's more to life than pollinating zucchinis by hand!

One sure-fire way to **attract pollinators** is to plant flowers that will bring them into your garden. Plant a lavender bush in a container and watch the bees buzz around it. Plant a few **flowers** here or there within your raised beds or containers. Although vegetable gardening purists may cringe at this idea, it's very much in keeping with English cottage gardening, where a variety of edibles and ornamentals flourish next to each other.

And it's not just flowers. Pollinators also relish herbs, so let some of your **herbs** like rosemary and oregano produce flowers; the pollinators will repay you in kind!

Bees and butterflies attracted to Verbena

9. Pests be gone! Organic alternatives for pest control

Before I explore the role of organic alternatives to chemicals in controlling pests, I need to review a couple of the most common bugs. These pests are mentioned in the quick-reference growing guides in chapter 6. You will need to be able to recognize them so that you can take care of the problem.

One of the most common pests is that of **aphids**. They thrive on *succulent new growth* and they suck the 'life-blood' out of the plant; a horticultural version of a tick! They come in a variety of colors and attack a broad spectrum of plants. They are particularly partial to the new shoots on roses.

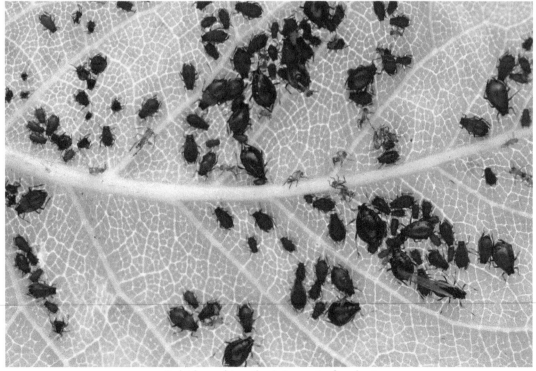

Aphids sucking the juice out of a plant

Tomato hookworm caterpillar on a tomato plant

Red spider mites are so minuscule that you may need a magnifying glass to see them. They often appear as webbing, and the plant will be noticeably distressed.

Another 'baddie' is the **tomato hookworm caterpillar**, but watch out for it on your peppers, potatoes, and eggplant as well.

Stink bugs damage tomatoes, beans and green peppers, but will also attack fruit trees and ornamentals.

The list of bugs is long, and I've just scratched the surface. Before you go screaming into the night, help is at hand: **Beneficial (predator) insects** are a powerful tool in the gardener's arsenal. They include the well-known ladybugs (ladybirds in the UK) and the lesser-known lacewings, and wasps among others. They will protect your harvest by preying on the bad insects - the *good guys vs the bad*!

Stink bugs live up to their name

Praying Mantis devouring a grasshopper

It's not just the praying mantis that is the gardener's little helper, but wasps play their part by laying their eggs on the tomato hookworm caterpillar; when the eggs hatch, they feed on the caterpillar host. Gross, but effective!

Ladybugs do their bit by eating aphids and also red spider mites.

While you can purchase beneficial insects, it is far better to attract them to your garden by creating the right conditions. Grow a wide range of plants and it will draw them. *It's a case of "build a garden and they will come"*.

Even though there is this army of helpers at hand, it still pays to be vigilant and act promptly at the first sign of a pest; don't wait for them to become an infestation. If you notice aphids, try **blasting** them with a really *hard* spray of water. You will find that a lot will drown.

You could also spray them with a solution of **dishwashing* liquid**. Start with a solution of 2.5 TBL soap and 2.5 TBL vegetable oil, mixed with 1 gallon of warm, not hot, water. Using a spray bottle, spray onto the aphids during the cool of the day. Always test on a plant before using on the entire crop. (*In the USA, Daisy dishwashing liquid is widely used for this.)

If all else fails, then choose an **organic pesticide**, like insecticidal soap or neem oil; they act by smothering the pests. Avoid spraying plants when they are flowering, and use in the early evening when bees are less active.

A final word of warning: Be careful of using **weed killer** beyond the raised bed. You run the risk of chemicals contaminating your edibles.

It pays to be **proactive**. You can avoid many pests by protecting your crops with '*row cover*'. You will see this referenced often in the growing guides in chapter 6. You can either make the hoops yourself (see chapter 2) or buy them. Drape the row cover over the hoops and secure with 'earth staples'.

Row cover provides protection against pests and excessive cold

Remember, healthy plants are more likely to shrug off adversity than a plant that has been allowed to become stressed. Feed your plants regularly, water effectively, and maintain your plants so that they are in tip-top shape. Encourage predator insects to your garden.

10. Maintenance, but not 'high' maintenance

Get into the habit of making a *daily* check of the garden. Involve the whole family if you can. **Pull out any weeds** before they become established. They too will thrive in your wonderful soil mix!

Remove, or '*deadhead*' any faded flowers. Don't let your herbs go to seed; pinch out the growing tips of basil, and cut off the flowering stems of herbs like marjoram and thyme. Keep a vigilant eye on plants that appear distressed. Look for signs of wind damage – perhaps a broken stem. Do you need to stake a plant, or do some tying up? Pick up any fruit that may have dropped to the ground. If you notice marks on leaves, remove them – they won't magically heal!

Don't let weeds get out of hand!

11. Will my garden tools break the bank?

The good news is that "*No, they* won't". Here's a handy list of what you'll need:

A selection of garden tools

- **Garden trowel** - look for an ergonomic handle
- **Hand cultivator** – two or three-pronged
- **Garden gloves**
- **Pruners**, aka, secateurs or pruning shears
- **Watering wand, watering can**, and **hose with adjustable spray head**
- **Plant tags and permanent marker**
- **Rake** for leveling raised beds
- **Spray bottle** (optional)
- **Wheelbarrow** (optional)

12. Some other horticultural bits and bobs

No gardening book would be complete without a description of a few key *gardening terms*:

Soil pH - Soil pH is how acidity and alkalinity are measured on a scale of 1 – 14, with 7 being the midpoint. The numbers below 7 are considered **acidic** and the numbers above **alkaline.**

For most plants, **5.5 – 6.5** is the sweet spot. Blueberries are an exception to this – they require a strongly acidic soil of 4.2 – 5.2 to succeed.

Although widely available, I don't recommend that the beginner gardener buy a pH meter. If you are concerned about your soil, then consider contacting your County Extension office for help. You want to be careful before you start messing with the pH.

Annuals vs perennials - There are quite a few herbs that are **annuals**, which means that they will complete their life cycle, and then they die. It's not because you've killed them, it's simply that they have a *short life expectancy* of less than a year. Basil, dill and cilantro are examples. Parsley falls into this category, although strictly speaking it's a biennial.

Sage, rosemary and thyme, on the other hand, are **perennials.** They are good value plants as they live for more than two years. Some *herbaceous* perennials, like peonies, go *dormant* in winter and die down completely. Using **plant tags**, with the plant's name written on it in permanent marker, is a useful way to remember where you planted herbaceous plants.

Heirlooms vs Hybrids - An **heirloom** is a plant variety that's been around for at least 50 years - think of it as the horticultural equivalent of an antique. In the world of tomatoes, there are lots of sought-after heirloom varieties, for example, 'Juliet', a lovely grape tomato. Heirlooms are highly prized for their flavor, although not always for their vigor.

That's where **hybrids** come in: They were bred to make the plants easier to grow by being more disease resistant, more uniform, often with higher yields.

Which is preferable? One is not necessarily better than the other. Heirlooms and hybrids bring different things to the table.

You now have a good grasp of gardening basics. Let's take a closer look at what's involved in sowing seeds.

Chapter 4

Life Begins with a Seed

How to Grow Plants from Seeds

The love of gardening is a seed once sown that never dies.
~Gertrude Jekyll

Remember to always read the seed packet carefully – it will have specific instructions for each plant.

The quick-reference growing guides in chapter 6 also provide information on how to sow seed.

This chapter takes a closer look at how to sow seed successfully.

There are two basic methods of sowing seed:

- **Sowing direct** is where seed is sown directly *'in situ'* in your container or raised bed

- **Indoor sowing** is where seed is started indoors.

Let's look at each of these methods in more detail:

1. Sowing direct

The best thing about sowing seed directly **in the ground** is that you don't have to bother with seed pots and other seed-growing equipment. Another plus is that you don't have to transplant the seedlings and run the risk of losing them.

The downside is that you can't control the elements. A heavy downpour could wash away your seed or drown your seedlings. Birds are also very partial to eating pea and sweet pea seeds.

Here is a simple step-by-step guide to sowing seed outdoors:

Planting cilantro seed in a furrow

Step 1: If you are using the **row method** in a container or raised bed, then make a narrow 'furrow' – the correct depth according to the seed packet. Sow the seed *thinly and evenly* along the furrow. Cover the seed lightly, unless the seed packet says not to.

If you are using the raised bed square-foot method, then sow small *'pockets'* of 3 seeds according to how many plants you can grow in a square foot, spacing the pockets out appropriately. For example, you can grow 4 spinach plants in a square foot. Space out the 'pockets' equidistant from each other inside the square. (See square-foot gardening for raised beds in chapter 5.)

Step 2: Maintain the level of moisture – don't let the top inch dry out – that's where the seed is. Aim for a little dampness, but the soil shouldn't be soggy. Water very gently; select the 'shower' setting on your hose attachment.

Step 3: When the seedlings are 2–3 inches tall and have at least 2 sets of leaves, **thin them out**. If more than one seed has germinated in a pocket, then you need to remove all but the strongest seedling.

Square-foot raised bed with seedlings clearly labeled

The best way to do this is by *snipping off* the other seedlings with scissors. If you pull out the unwanted plants, you run the risk of disturbing the best seedling.

Step 4: Use plant labels to indicate the plant variety and sowing date. It's very easy to forget.

2. Indoor sowing

The main reason why seed is started indoors is because it is too cold outdoors for the seed to germinate. Indoor sowing gives your crops a *jump-start*.

When to sow indoors? You want to start your vegetable seed indoors in **early spring** – February/March - so that you can plant them out as soon as *all danger of frost has passed.* As a general rule of thumb, sow indoors about 6–8 weeks before your last spring frost date for your zone. See chapter 5 for a discussion on zones.

What equipment do you need to sow seed indoors? You will have to invest in some equipment. You will need something in which to plant your seeds. There are different ways of doing this:

Pepper plants growing thickly in a seed tray

Seed trays are a very economical way of starting seed. When the seedlings reach a certain stage, they are either 'potted on' (repotted) into individual pots, or they are transplanted outside into the container or raised bed.

Transplanting seedlings can be challenging; they will suffer from some degree of setback as a result of being transplanted. This is not a viable method for plants that have a deep taproot and won't tolerate disturbance, like carrots and beets.

A better method is to sow seed directly into **individual pots**. These pots may be separate (stand-alone), or joined together in packs of varying sizes.

When the plant is big enough, you would take it out of the pot, *without disturbing the roots*, and put it in its permanent position.

An even better option is to use a *peat pot*, or biodegradable pot, for each seed. The beauty of this method is that you plant the *entire peat pot with seedling* into the soil, with no root disturbance. The roots will grow through the peat pot; you don't remove it.

12-pack seed tray

Cucumber seedlings showing roots emerging through the peat pot

What makes pots so great? When transplanting a seedling you want to do everything possible to avoid *'transplant shock'*. Transplanted properly, the plant should not even know it's been relocated! This gives peat pots a huge advantage over individual pots.

Invoking the mantra of *quality over quantity* again, I strongly advocate investing in pots, rather than trays. You don't want to put time and effort into sowing indoors, only to lose these seedlings when you transplant them. And if your budget stretches to peat pots, so much the better!

The correct seed-growing medium To sow seeds successfully, you will need a sterilized soil mix formulated for starting seeds; it should be very light, and allow the roots to penetrate easily, while retaining moisture.

Baby, it's warm in here! It's important to provide warmth for germinating the seeds. **Heat mats** are often used to boost germination.

In addition, many gardeners use **grow-lights** to simulate sunlight which seedlings need to grow. Grow-lights run the gamut from DIY options to highly sophisticated, multi-tiered stacking systems. However, they all share one common feature; they bring the sunshine indoors. If you are considering buying a grow-light, then look at the LED and fluorescent models – they are a good starting point. You can always 'grow' bigger.

By the way, grow-lights are not only great for germinating seeds, but they can also be used for growing fresh herbs indoors, not to mention microgreens – vegetable greens that are harvested when they are very immature, and which have become very trendy.

Seed starter kits are also available. One of the more interesting options includes a humidifier, reservoir, jumbo cells and special peat pots.

Multiple lettuce seed germinating in most seed compartments

Here is a simple step-by-step guide to sowing seed indoors:

Step 1: *Moisten your seed-sowing medium*; it should be damp, but not sodden.

Step 2: *Read the instructions on the seed packet.* It will tell you how deep to plant the seed. Occasionally, you will find that some seeds should not be covered, as they need light to germinate.

Step 3: I use a pencil (chopstick will work too) to *make a small hole* in the center of the pot. (I will have already marked up the pencil, with a permanent pen, with lines indicating ⅛, ¼, ½ and 1 inch.)

Step 4: Not all seeds will germinate. Drop 2 – 3 seeds into each of the holes in the pot.

Step 5: Cover lightly with the same sowing medium, unless the seed packet indicates otherwise.

Step 6: Using a spray bottle, *gently* mist the seed pots.

Step 7: Use plant labels to indicate plant variety and sowing date.

Step 8: Check the seeds every day. The moment they germinate, they will need light. This could be as simple as placing the pots on your windowsill or using a **grow-light.**

Step 9: If more than one seed has germinated, then you need to remove all but the strongest plant. Thin out when the seedlings are about 2 – 3 inches tall and have 2 sets of leaves.

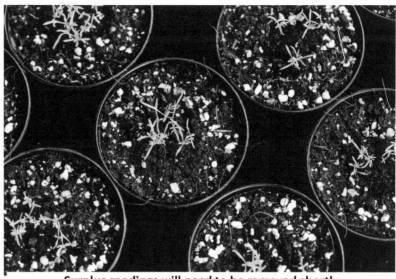
Surplus seedings will need to be removed shortly

The best way to do this is by snipping off the other seedlings with scissors. If you pull out the unwanted plants, you run the risk of disturbing the best seedling.

Step 10: Seedlings will follow the light. If you're growing your seedlings on a windowsill, then rotate them daily. Otherwise, they will end up growing at a weird angle. If you're using a grow-light then position the seedlings very close to the light. If you forget to do this, they will grow long and 'leggy' as they reach for the sun! Lanky plants are undesirable.

Step 11: When your seedlings are about 3 – 4" tall, and after all danger of frost has passed, it's time to get them ready to go outside. You will need to acclimate them to the outdoors; you can't just plant them out straightaway. Ideally, you want to put them outside in filtered shade - under a tree is perfect. The goal is to '**harden'** them off to growing outdoors. Leave them outdoors for a few hours at a time – but *not overnight*. Repeat the process for a few days, gradually lengthening the time that they are outdoors. Each day expose them to more sunshine. This should ensure that are ready for planting in their 'forever' home.

Tomato seedlings growing on a windowsill

Step 12: When you transplant the pot into your container or raised bed, keep it at the same level. The only exception to this is tomatoes, which should be planted a little deeper; they will actually develop roots from the newly submerged stem.

> Keep a garden journal - record when you sowed seed, planted out the seedlings, and fertilized them. This will be an invaluable record for future years.

Is starting plants from seed worth the time and money? One of the benefits of sowing your own seed is that seed catalogs offer a far bigger **choice of varieties** than you would find at a garden center. This is important since varieties do differ in significant ways: Some varieties are *bush* varieties and quite *dwarf*, others are *vining* varieties that climb and require support. Some are more *'disease-resistant'* than others. For example, some tomato varieties are less likely to suffer from 'blossom-end rot'. Some varieties are better suited to dealing with *heat or cold*. Consider these factors when making your selection. It's very easy to get carried away when ordering seeds - we've all done this!

If you can't plant the seed straight away, store it in a sealed envelope in the refrigerator (not freezer). Include a pack of silica gel to keep the seeds dry. Write the date on the seed packet; it won't last forever! Parsley seed is notorious for having a short shelf-life – it needs to be sown fresh.

Volunteers! No discussion on seeds would be complete without mentioning plants that self-sow; the plant goes to seed, seeds drift here and there, eventually the seed germinates and 'voila' you have a 'volunteer' plant!

While it is tempting to save money by collecting your own seed, there are a few things you should know about seeds. If you grew fancy F1 hybrid tomatoes and you thought you could collect some seed for the following year, not so fast. F1 hybrids will not come true the following year. The tomatoes may well be very nice, but they definitely won't be the same as the original F1 hybrid.

If you do want to collect your own seed, make sure that the seed is ready: If you open a seed pod, you will see that the seed is green. It will usually change color when it is ready to harvest. The seed pod will split open when the seed is ripe. Sometimes the seed pod can disgorge its seed very quickly and you will find the seed all gone. A solution is to cover the seed pod with a stocking, or tights, to trap the seed.

I like to let some of my basil and parsley plants go to seed. When the seed is ready, I just sprinkle it over my containers, and when the time is right, it will germinate. I try to let them grow where they come up; they always seem happier if left alone to grow where they will.

One of the great pleasures in life for the keen gardener is perusing a seed catalog. Whether or not you sow seed indoors or directly 'in situ', there is something very magical about growing a plant from seed to table. Let's start planning your garden.

Chapter 5

It's All Part of the Plan

Successful Gardeners Follow a Plan

One of the most delightful things about a garden is the anticipation it provides.
~W.E. Johns, The Passing Show

Since you are gardening in a defined area, be it containers or a raised bed, you want to make the most of every square inch available to you.

The successful gardener plans their garden ahead of time.

*This chapter explores the techniques that you can utilize to maximize your harvest when **planning your garden**.*

1. A plant in every nook and cranny! Interplanting

Traditionally large slower-growing plants like tomatoes are grown in solitary splendor, even though they take a fairly long time to reach their full height. The canny urban gardener recognizes that the space around the tomato is being under-utilized for the first month of its life, and *plants smaller, quick-growing vegetables around it.* By the time the tomato reaches its full potential, the smaller plants, which include radishes and salad greens, have long been harvested and removed.

This clever harvest-boosting method is known as **interplanting**. Not only will it increase your available planting space, but it will also *reduce your water bill.* The taller plants provide shade for the low growing plants around them, and prevent the ground from drying out so quickly. Incorporate interplanting into your garden plan.

Plants growing closely in an elevated raised bed

2. It's a relay race! Succession planting

Beginner gardeners often make the mistake of planting too many of the same variety at the same time, resulting in a glut of vegetables; there's only so much cabbage one can eat at one time! A much better method is to make small plantings every two to three weeks, so **they don't all mature at the same time**.

This staggered planting method also works well for cut flowers like gladiolus; you want to plant a container of bulbs ever two weeks to ensure that you have cut flowers for an extended period of time. This technique is called **succession planting.** You will see that I have implemented succession planting in the *three-season planting plan* at the end of the chapter.

You can also extend the season by **planting two to three crops in succession in the same space**. In the **early spring**, plant cool-season crops like broccoli, carrots, peas, spinach and lettuce. After harvesting them, amend the soil and in the **summer** follow with warm-season crops like tomatoes, cucumbers, peppers, beans and corn. Amend the soil and follow with a new batch of cool-season crops that can take some frost, like carrots, chard and cauliflower in the **fall** (autumn).

Make your gardening real estate work for you throughout the growing season; integrate succession planting in your garden plan.

3. Friends help friends! Companion planting

Closely related to interplanting is the concept of **companion planting,** that also maximizes available growing space.

Based in part on folklore, and perhaps not fully supported by science, companion planting suggests that certain plants can benefit from each other by increasing soil nutrients, attracting beneficial insects and pollinators, repelling pests, and even providing support - corn can be used as a living trellis for runner beans!

Marigolds growing among the vegetables

Bees cannot resist a lavender bush in flower

Flowers, like marigolds, nasturtiums and zinnias, are often grown as **friendly companions** interplanted among their vegetable cousins. Marigolds attract aphid-eating ladybugs. Zinnias are highly prized by pollinators, and a pot of lavender will have bees buzzing busily around it.

Utilize companion plants in your garden plan to maximize your harvest and *reduce pests and disease*.

4. 'Crop' around the clock! Crop rotation

Traditionally crops are grown in *strict rotation*, with a different 'family' of crops grown each year. There are three families: **Roots** (carrots, parsnips, etc.), **brassicas** (broccoli, kale, etc.), and **other** which includes everything else (beans, tomatoes, lettuce, etc.). Ideally, you would rotate through each of these three 'families', and then start again with a vegetable from the first family. **Crop rotation** is very important, because it restricts pests and prevents soil from being stripped of its nutrients.

However, *full-scale* crop rotation may not be feasible for the urban gardener. I suggest you follow this **simplified routine**:

First year: roots (carrots, parsnips, onions, etc.)

Next year: leafy vegetables grown for their *above-ground* harvest (kale, tomatoes, basil, etc.)

Incorporate this *modified crop rotation routine* into your garden plan.

5. The greenhouse effect! Extending the growing season

Another way of getting the greatest amount of harvest out of a relatively tight space is to **extend the growing season**. In colder areas where frost would literally nip your garden in the bud, you can stretch out the growing season by creating warmth for your plants.

This is quite easy to achieve. In Chapter 2, I explained how to make a **hoop house** using rebar. Essentially it is a frame to which you attach **row cover** or greenhouse plastic. If like me you are not DIY-inclined, ready-made hoop houses are conveniently available.

You can even create a mini-greenhouse effect by covering the frost-tender plant with a garden *'cloche'* as well – this is like a mini portable greenhouse that covers the plant. In the old days it was made of glass; today it is made of plastic. Just remember to remove these coverings once warmer days return.

Being able to extend your growing season by two to three weeks in the spring and the same in the fall, is a good reason for investing in a hoop house and incorporating this into your garden plan.

Garden cloche protects a tender plant from the elements

6. You're in the zone! The Plant Hardiness zone map

Finally, when planning your garden, get your bearings. In the United States, the **USDA Hardiness Zone map** enables US* gardeners to identify their **growing zone**, based on their zip code. The map is based on the average annual minimum winter temperature. (*International hardiness zones and their websites are listed at the back of the book.)

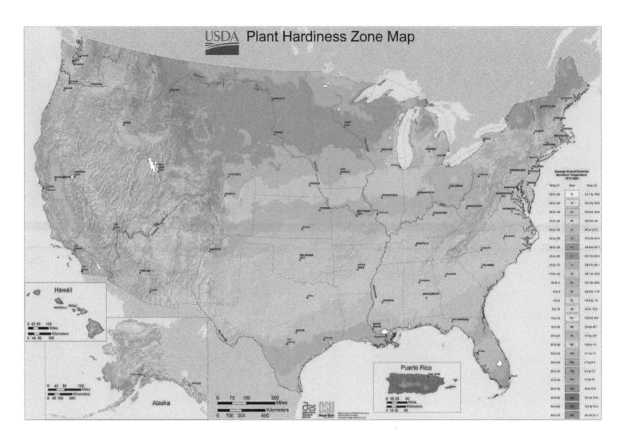

What's the big deal about your zone? Plants have pretty specific needs; sadly, *not all plants thrive in all zones.* For example, peonies are notoriously difficult to grow in zones 9 and higher. Tomatoes curl up their toes at the first really cold snap, and container-grown lemon trees are frost-sensitive.

How will I use this knowledge? You've studied the map and identified your growing zone. As you start **planning your garden**, always check on the plant's growing zone requirements – will it grow in your zone, and will it need protection against frost? Not only does your growing zone determine what plant you can grow, but also what variety of that plant is right for your area.

Ask your local nursery or county extension office for advice. If you have a short growing season because of your zone, select varieties that are early-maturing. Consider extending the growing season by using 'row cover'.

Information on growing zones is included in the growing guides in chapter 6.

Knowing your plant hardiness zone enables you to better plan your garden. Planning in turn leads to success.

7. Where, When, How and What!

Finally, when planning your garden, remember that some plants are better suited to growing in containers; others may be happier in a raised bed. Plants have different needs; some require cool conditions, while others need warmth to succeed. In this section, I will explain *where* to plant, *when* to plant, *how* to plant and *what* to plant.

The Where factor!

Vegetables that do well in containers: While the urban gardener can grow almost any edibles or ornamentals in a container, there are some that thrive when grown in a container.

Herbs, like basil, oregano, parsley, chives – the list goes on – do wonderfully well, even in quite small containers. Beans, eggplant, peppers, spinach, tomatoes and zucchini are summer staples for growing in containers, but will require more space. Beets, bok choy, broccoli, and chard are wonderful in the spring and fall garden, as are kale, peas and radishes. You can even grow carrots in a container, as long as you select a deep container; carrots need a depth of 12 inches.

Which container is right for my plants? For the gardener just starting out, it is very difficult to know what *size* container to use with which vegetable. Also, *how do you know how many plants* you can grow in one container without overcrowding them?

The following table – **Containers by size and plant capacity** – will enable you to:

- select the right size container for your edibles

- know how many plants you can grow in the container.

You will notice that circular containers, commonly called '*pots*', are measured by **diameter**.

Containers by size and plant capacity:

Size of Container	Plant	Number of plants
10-inch pot (25 cm)	Beans – bush variety	1
	Carrots	11 - 12
	Chard	1
	Leaf lettuce	1
	Strawberry	1
	Turnips	4
	Herbs - Chives, Parsley, Mint, Oregano, Sage	1
14-inch pot (36 cm)	Arugula	3 - 4
	Corn - dwarf variety	6 - 7
	Cabbage	1
	Carrots	9 - 10
	Leaf lettuce	3 - 4
	Peas	4
	Spinach	3 - 4
	Herbs, such as Rosemary and Lavender	1
16-inch pot (41 cm)	Beans - runner with support	3 - 4
	Dwarf citrus tree	1
	Blueberry – dwarf variety	1
18-inch pot (46 cm)	Beans - runner with support	4 - 6
	Broccoli	1
	Cauliflower	1
	Eggplant	1
	Pepper	1
	Determinate (bush) Tomato	1
24-inch pot (61 cm)	Indeterminate (vining) Tomato	1
	Cucumber	1
	Zucchini - Summer squash	1
	Apple – dwarf variety	1
30-inch pot (76 cm)	Sweet corn	1
	Pumpkin – bush type	1
	Rhubarb	1

Pots are sometimes sold by capacity:

Pot diameter (in inches)	Gallon	Liter
10	2½ - 3	9 - 11
14	6 - 7	23 - 26
16	9 - 10	23 - 26
18	14 - 15	53 - 75
24	24 - 25	91 - 95
30	30	114

How far apart do I space plants in a raised bed? One of the great mysteries facing beginner gardeners is *how far apart you should space your plants in the raised bed.*

Traditionally, gardeners used the information found on the back of seed packets, which dictated the **space between plants.** (It also gave the distance between rows, but as we've seen, that doesn't apply to gardening in raised beds.) We've already established that as a raised bed gardener you are in the enviable position of being able to **reduce** the space between plants, because you're using a super-rich growing medium.

You have two choices as to how to plant in your raised bed:

1. **Row planting:** As the name suggests, plants are grown *in rows – each variety is grown in its own row.* This is a very straightforward, uncomplicated method ideally suited to the beginner gardener.

Plants are grown in rows

Plants are grown in 12" squares

2. **Square foot gardening** is another option available to the raised bed gardener who is looking to *maximize the yield even more*.

Here's how it works: You divide your space into a grid of **1- x 1-foot** squares, using a *physical grid*. You can make a home-made grid out of wood lath or Venetian blinds. You can also use string to delineate the squares. With an 8' x 4' raised bed, you will have *32 squares available for planting*.

You then follow the **Square Foot Planting Guide** which tells you how many plants (or seeds) will fit in each square. It's all based on the *ultimate* size of the plant; the smaller the plant, the more you can fit into the square. For example, you can fit 16 carrots in a square, compared to 1 tomato.

For a really neat two-in-one product, try the **Garden Grid™ Watering Systems**, which is a plant spacing guide and pre-assembled garden watering system all in one!

So, what's the benefit of square foot gardening? This highly intensive block method works extremely well for the urban garden where space is at an absolute premium. Using this method, every square inch is utilized.

Which method is better? There's no question that square foot gardening is a 'super-efficient' method, and more and more raised bed gardeners are turning to it. However, perhaps you prefer the simplicity of the row method. It's your raised bed; you need to do what feels right for you.

You will be able to plan how many plants you need for your raised bed by using the following **planting and spacing chart.** It works for both the *square foot* and *row method.*

The When factor! Cool- and Warm-season plants

Vegetables and herbs are divided into two groups: cool- and warm-season. **Cool-season** plants are grown in *spring* and *fall*. Not surprisingly, **warm-season** plants are grown during *summer*. When you're planning your garden, you need to know which plant prefers which season. You will see that the planting and spacing chart is divided into cool-season plants and warm-season plants.

The How factor! How to space your plants and how long do they take to mature?

You will also need to know how long vegetables and herbs take to mature. The length of time that a plant takes, from the time the seed is sown to the harvesting of the crop, is called **days-to-harvest.** You will find this helpful when planning your garden. This information is in the right-hand column of the chart.

Planting & Spacing Chart: Cool-season Vegetables and Herbs

Cool-season Vegetables	Row Method Space between plants (in inches)	Square Foot Method Plants per square foot	Days to Maturity
Beans – fava (broad bean)	8 - 10	4	75 - 85
Beets	2 - 4	9	50 - 70
Bok Choi	8 - 10	4	45 - 50
Broccoli	12 - 18	1	50 - 65
Brussel sprouts	15 - 18	1	100 - 140
Cabbage	15 - 18	1	60 - 90
Carrots	2 - 3	16	60 - 80
Cauliflower	15 - 18	1	55 - 80
Chinese Cabbage	10 - 12	8	80
Chard	6 - 9	4	45 - 55
Green onions (Spring onions/ Scallions)	9	16	55 - 65
Kale	15 - 18	2	55 - 65
Leek	6 - 9	6	120 - 150
Lettuce – head	10 - 12	2	45 - 60
Lettuce – leaf	4	16	35 - 55
Onion	2 - 4	9	100 - 142
Parsnips	2 - 4	9	110 - 130
Peas	2 - 4	9	55 - 85
Potatoes	2 - 18	2	90 - 120
Radish	2 - 3	16	25 - 40
Rhubarb	30 - 36	1	1 - 2 year
Shallots	4 - 6	4	90
Spinach	4 - 6	9	45 - 60
Strawberries	12	4	1 year
Turnips	4 - 6	9	40 - 60
Herbs:			
Chives	8	4	80
Cilantro	8	4	65
Dill	8	4	60
Parsley	10 - 12	4	80
Sage	20 - 25	1	70s
Thyme	10	4	80

Planting & Spacing Chart: Warm-season Vegetables and Herbs

Warm-season Vegetables	Row Method Space between plants (in inches)	Square Foot Method Plants per square foot	Days to Maturity
Beans - bush, Beans - pole (runner)	4 - 6 6 - 12	4 6	55 - 65
Chinese cabbage	10 - 12	8	60 - 80
Corn	15 - 18	2	70 - 105
Cucumber	12 - 18	1	55 - 65
Eggplant (Aubergine/Brinjal)	18 - 24	1	75 - 90
Melons - Cantaloupe	18 - 24	1 per 2 squares	75 - 100
Peppers – bell and hot	12 - 15	1	60 - 90
Pumpkin	24 - 36	1	85 - 120
Sweet potatoes	12 - 18	1	100 - 125
Tomatoes	18 - 24	1	65 - 90
Watermelon	24 -o 72	1 per 2 squares	80 - 100
Winter squash -	36	1	85 - 120
Zucchini (Summer squash / Courgettes)	18 - 24	1	50 - 60
Herbs:			
Basil	12 - 15	2 - 4	70
Oregano	15 - 20	2	85

The What factor!

Vegetables that give you bang for your buck! Not surprisingly, most beginner gardeners will be spurred on by quick results. I highly recommend trying the following vegetables, which you can bring to your table in less than a month:

Vegetables That Give You BANG For Your BUCK!

Arugula
Beans - Bush Variety
Bok Choy
Carrot - Baby
Green Onions
Lettuce: Cut-Again Leaves
Kale: Cut Baby Leaves
Radish
Spinach

Cut flowers that wow! Here are 10 wonderful cut flowers that will grow in a container. Pop a few marigolds in your raised bed to ward away the 'baddies'.

Cut Flowers That WOW!

Alstroemeria
Cosmos
Dahilia
Freesia
Lavender
Lily
Marigold
Rose
Sweet Pea
Zinnia

It's time to plan your garden!

You now have all the information that you need to **plan** your container or raised bed garden.

Follow the #1 rule: **Plant what your family loves to eat**. Sounds simple doesn't it, but often we're tempted to plant on a whim, with the family being less than inspired!

Remember that some crops like cool conditions, while others thrive in the warmth of summer.

Choose varieties that suit your zone. If your growing season is not very long, select varieties that have a shorter growing season. Start them inside from seed as early as your zone allows; or buy starter plants that will save you valuable growing time. Consider extending your growing season with row covers.

By applying these principles, the savvy gardener can plan for three successive crops:

In *early* **spring** plant *cool-weather* crops. Follow this with *warm-weather* sun lovers in **summer**; complete the growing season by planting *cool-weather* crops again in the **fall**.

I will show you how to get three successive crops out of one raised bed, using the square-foot method; truly making it worth the investment!

The 8' by 4' raised bed is orientated *north to south*, with a trellis structure at the northern end, in the northern hemisphere. Tall plants are situated at the northern end, with the lowest growing plants at the southern end; all plants receive the maximum amount of sun.

> **To avoid damaging the roots, stake your plant when the seedling is small.**

Certain plants, like strawberries and some of the herbs, like sage, are perennials and are permanent fixtures in the bed. Others, like tomatoes, peas, cabbage, leek and onions, occupy two seasons, as they are slow to mature. You could interplant among these when they are still young plants.

Amend the soil between crops.

For each season I have provided the **number of plants** needed using the *square foot* method:

The Three-Season Planting Plan: Spring

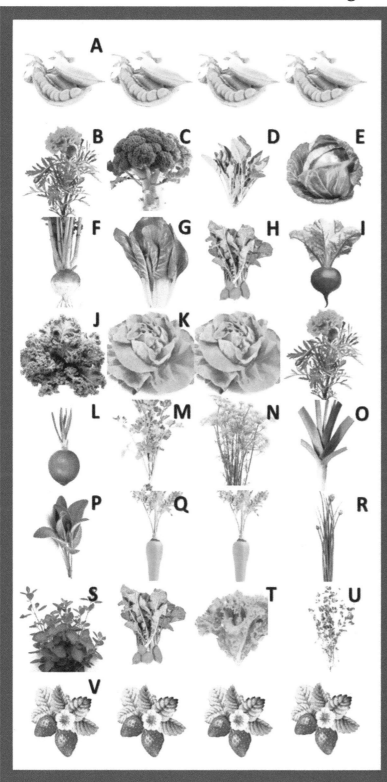

A   36 peas (4 squares)

B   4 marigolds (2 squares)

C   1 broccoli

D   9 spinach

E   1 cabbage

F   9 turnips

G   4 chard

H   32 radishes (2 squares)
plant 2nd square two weeks later

I   9 beets

J   2 kale

K   4 lettuce (2 squares)
plant 2nd square two weeks later

L   9 onions

M   4 parsley

N   4 dill

O   6 leeks

P   1 sage (perennial)

Q   32 carrots (2 squares)
plant 2nd square two weeks later

R   4 chives (perennial)

S   1 oregano (perennial)
start later

T   16 leaf lettuce

U   4 thyme (perennial)

V   16 strawberry (perennial) (4 squares)

The Three-Season Planting Plan: Summer

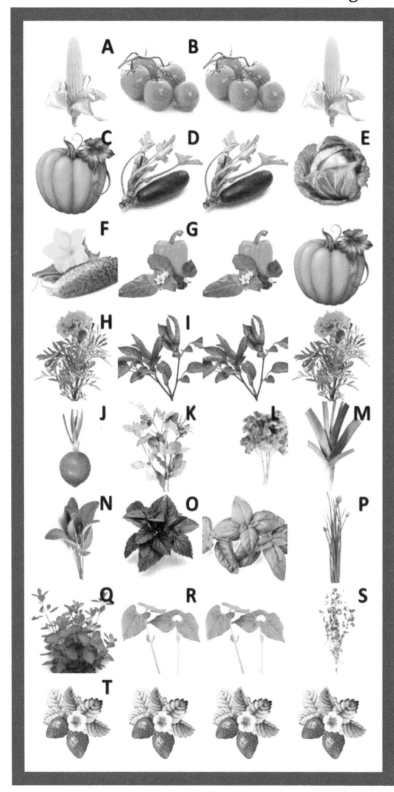

A 4 corn (2 squares)
plant 2nd square two weeks later

B 2 tomatoes (2 squares)

C 2 winter squash
(2 squares)
plant 2nd square two weeks later

D 2 zucchinis (2 squares)
plant 2nd square two weeks later

E 1 cabbage
- *yet to be harvested*

F 1 cucumber

G 2 bell peppers
(2 squares)

H 4 marigolds (2 squares)

I 2 hot peppers
(2 squares)

J 9 onions
- *yet to be harvested*

K 2 Thai basil

L 4 parsley

M 6 leeks
- *yet to be harvested*

N 1 sage (perennial)

O 4 basil (2 squares)

P 4 chives (perennial)

Q 1 oregano (perennial)

R 8 bush beans
(2 squares)

S 4 thyme (perennial)

T 16 strawberry
(perennial) (4 squares)

The Three-Season Planting Plan: Fall (Autumn)

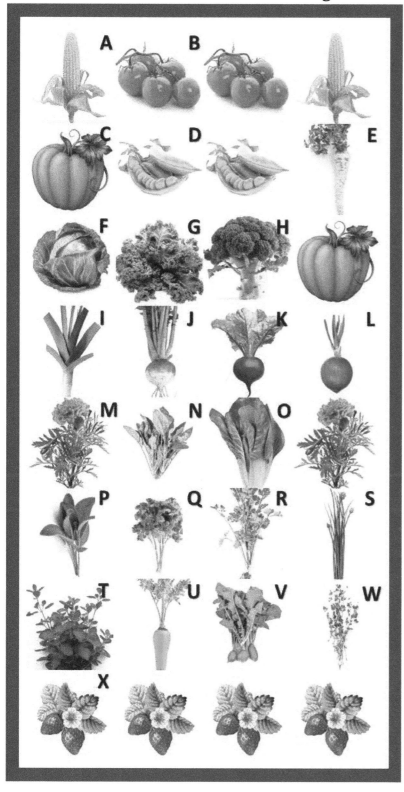

A 4 corn (2 squares)
   - *still being harvested*

B 2 tomatoes (2 squares)
   - *still being harves*ted

C 2 winter squash
   (2 squares) -
   not yet harvested

D 18 peas (2 squares)

E 9 parsnips

F 1 cabbage

G 2 kale

H 1 broccoli

I 6 leeks

J 9 turnips

K 9 beets

L 9 onions

M 4 marigolds (2 squares)

N 9 spinach

O 4 chard

P 1 sage (perennial)

Q 4 parsley

R 4 cilantro

S 4 chives (perennial)

T 1 oregano (perennial)

U 16 carrots

V 16 radishes

W 4 thyme (perennial)

X 16 strawberry
   (perennial) (4 squares)

Small space urban gardening is all about getting the most you possibly can out of your containers or raised bed. Applying these techniques will empower you to achieve this goal.

After the last harvest in fall, remember to amend your soil mix by topdressing with a 2-inch layer of mulch to prepare your raised bed for the following spring bounty.

In the next chapter, we will look at growing guides for a wide range of edibles and ornamentals.

Chapter 6

Grow Your Garden to Success

How to Grow Vegetables, Herbs, Fruit and Cut Flowers

When weeding, the best way to make sure you are removing a weed and not a valuable plant is to pull on it. If it comes out of the ground easily, it is a valuable plant.
~Author unknown

This chapter presents quick-reference growing guides for a wide range of edibles and ornamentals.

They are color-coded to facilitate accessibility:

Vegetables	*yellow*
Herbs	*green*
Fruit	*lilac*
Cut-flowers	*pink*

The quick-reference growing guides will further enhance your ability to plan your garden successfully.

How to interpret the quick-reference growing guides

- The height of the plant, as well as the days-to-maturity, is often given as **a range**. Varieties of the same plant may differ. Always look for a variety that works for your zone and suits your needs

- **Exposure** indicates whether the plant should be grown in full sun, semi-shade or shade

- Not all plants are cultivated from **seed**; they may be grown from a bulb or a root. This applies particularly to cut flowers

- Given the choice, buy **potted up fruit trees and roses** rather than *bareroot stock*. Bareroot stock plants would arrive without a pot and would need to be planted immediately. Special care needs to be taken when planting them out; the potted version offers a much greater guarantee of success

- The **ease-of-care** refers to how easy it is to cultivate a plant – this ranges from *easy* (1) to *challenging* (5).

Always read the plant label and take note of the instructions on the seed packet. They both provide valuable advice for that plant variety.

The information in the following quick-reference growing guides will give you additional tools to grow your garden in containers and raised beds.

GROWING GUIDE: ARUGULA (Rocket)			
Plant type	Annual	Seed to harvest (in days)	30 - 40
Frost tolerant	Somewhat	Seed planting depth (inches)	Barely cover seed
Zones (USDA)	3 - 10	Sow method	Direct sow
Exposure	Full sun to part shade	When to sow seed inside	-
Season	Cool	When to sow seed outdoors	4 weeks before last frost *in situ*
Height (inches)	8"- 12"	Germination time (in days)	5 - 7
Ease-of-care	1		
Problems	Protect plants from flea beetles, cabbage loopers and birds with a floating row cover. Watch for slugs.		
Comments	Don't allow the soil to dry out. For a continuous supply, plant every 2 – 3 weeks.		

GROWING GUIDE: BEANS

Plant type	Annual – Bush and Vine varieties	Seed to harvest (in days)	45 - 55
Frost tolerant	No	Seed planting (inches)	1 inch
Zones (USDA)	3 - 10	Sow method	Direct sow preferred
Exposure	Full sun	When to sow seed inside	3-4 weeks before last frost date
Season	Warm	When to sow seed outdoors	Directly after last frost *in situ*
Height (inches)	12" - 72"	Germination time (in days)	6 - 10
Ease-of-care	2		
Problems	Aphids – use a strong jet of water to blast them off.		
Comments	Transplant with care. Avoid watering foliage. Pole (runner) beans varieties will require support. 'Mascotte' & 'Tender Crop' are good varieties for a small space.		

BEETS			
Plant type	Annual	Seed to harvest (in days)	50 - 65
Frost tolerant	Yes	Seed planting depth (inches)	¼ to ½ inch
Zones (USDA)	3 - 10	Sow method	Sow direct/indoor sow
Exposure	Full sun	When to sow seed inside	4 weeks before last frost
Season	Cool	When to sow seed outdoors	4 weeks before last frost *in situ*
Height (inches)	4" - 12"	Germination time (in days)	5 - 15
Ease-of-care	3		
Problems	Protect plants from leaf miners with a floating row cover.		
Comments	Soak the seed in warm (not boiling) water for 24 hours before sowing. Each seed will germinate 2 – 4 seeds. Thin out carefully and harvest young leaves. Pick between 40 – 50 days for tender beets. 'Detroit Dark Red Medium' is a good variety for a small space.		

GROWING GUIDE: BROCCOLI			
Plant type	Annual	**Seed to harvest (in days)**	65 - 75
Frost tolerant	Yes	**Seed planting depth (inches)**	¼ to ½ inch
Zones (USDA)	3 - 10	**Sow method**	Direct sow/indoor sow
Exposure	Full sun	**When to sow seed inside**	5 - 6 weeks before last frost
Season	Cool & Warm	**When to sow seed outdoors**	Mid-late summer
Height (inches)	18"- 36"	**Germination time (in days)**	4 - 14
Ease-of-care	4		
Problems	Aphids – use a strong jet of water to blast them off. Protect plants from cabbage worm and flea beetles with a floating row cover.		
Comments	Avoid growing in mid-summer as the heat will cause it to bolt. 'DeCicco' & 'Green Comet' are good varieties for a small space.		

GROWING GUIDE: CABBAGE

Plant type	Annual	Seed to harvest (in days)	50 - 70
Frost tolerant	Yes	Seed planting depth (inches)	¼ to ½ inch
Zones (USDA)	1 - 10	Sow method	Direct sow/indoor sow
Exposure	Full sun	When to sow seed inside	6 weeks before last frost
Season	Cool	When to sow seed outdoors	Spring
Height (inches)	12" - 24"	Germination time (in days)	4 - 14
Ease-of-care	4 - 5		
Problems	Aphids – use a strong jet of water to blast them off. Protect plants from flea beetles and cabbage worms with a floating row cover.		
Comments	They have very shallow root systems. Avoid cultivating around them. Avoid wetting foliage. 'Golden Acres' & 'Tiara' are good varieties for a small space.		

GROWING GUIDE: CARROTS

Plant type	Annual	Seed to harvest (days)	45 - 75
Frost tolerant	Yes	Seed planting depth (inches)	¼ to ½ inch
Zones (USDA)	3 - 10	Sow method	Direct sow
Exposure	Full sun	When to sow seed inside	-
Season	Cool	When to sow seed outdoors	4 weeks before last frost *in situ*
Height (inches)	12" - 20"	Germination time (in days)	7 - 21
Ease-of-care	3		
Problems	Protect plants from carrot fly with a floating row cover.		
Comments	Thin out seedling by cutting with scissors to prevent carrot fly attack. Carrots are deep-rooted and need a soil depth of 12" to develop fully. 'Yaya Organic', 'Paris Market' & 'Little Finger' are good varieties for a small space.		

GROWING GUIDE: CHARD (Swiss Chard)			
Plant type	Annual	**Seed to harvest (days)**	55 - 70
Frost tolerant	Somewhat	**Seed planting depth (inches)**	½ inch
Zones (USDA)	3 - 10	**Sow method**	Direct sow/indoor sow
Exposure	Full - partial sun	**When to sow seed inside**	6 weeks before last frost
Season	Cool	**When to sow seed outdoors**	4 weeks before last frost *in situ*
Height (inches)	12" - 30"	**Germination time (in days)**	5 - 7
Ease-of-care	1		
Problems	Aphids – use a strong jet of water to blast them off. Protect plants from leaf miners with a floating row cover.		
Comments	Like beets, each chard seed produces more than one plant – thin out seedlings. 'Bright Lights' is a good variety for a small space.		

GROWING GUIDE: CORN			
Plant type	Annual	**Seed to harvest (in days)**	75 - 90
Frost tolerant	No	**Seed planting depth (inches)**	1 - 2 inch
Zones (USDA)	3 - 10	**Sow method**	Direct sow/ indoor sow
Exposure	Full sun	**When to sow seed inside**	2 – 3 weeks before last frost
Season	Warm	**When to sow seed outdoors**	2 – 3 weeks after last frost
Height (inches)	48" - 96"	**Germination time (in days)**	4 - 10
Ease-of-care	4		
Problems	Rust – avoid wetting foliage. Plant early to avoid earworm.		
Comments	Look for **disease-resistant varieties**. Needs very fertile soil -grow where peas or beans were grown previously to boost nitrogen levels in the soil. Intercrop with early harvest cool-season crops. 'On Deck' & 'Blue Jade' are good varieties for a small space.		

GROWING GUIDE: CUCUMBER

Plant type	Annual: – bush and vine varieties	Seed to harvest (in days)	50 - 70
Frost tolerant	No	Seed planting depth (inches)	½ to ¾ inch
Zones (USDA)	2 - 10	Sow method	Direct sow/indoor sow
Exposure	Full sun	When to sow seed inside	6 weeks before last frost
Season	Warm	When to sow seed outdoors	4 weeks after last frost
Height (inches)	12" - 72"'	Germination time (in days)	7 - 10
Ease-of-care	3		
Problems	Aphids – use a strong jet of water to blast them off. Protect plants from squash bugs and cucumber beetles with a floating row cover. Mildew – avoid watering the leaves.		
Comments	Grow **mildew-resistant varieties**, if possible. Bush varieties are ideally suited for containers. Vine varieties will require support. 'Miniature White', 'Bush Pickle' & 'Spacemaster 80' are good varieties for a small space.		

GROWING GUIDE: GREEN ONIONS			
(Bunching onion, Scallion, Spring onion, Welsh onion)			
Plant type	Annual	**Seed to harvest (in days)**	55 - 110
Frost tolerant	Somewhat	**Seed planting depth (inches)**	¼ inch
Zones (USDA)	5 - 9	**Sow method**	Direct sow/Indoor sow
Exposure	Full sun	**When to sow seed inside**	5 - 6 weeks before last frost
Season	Cool	**When to sow seed outdoors**	After all danger of frost is past
Height (inches)	12" - 30"	**Germination time (in days)**	7 - 10
Ease-of-care	2		
Problems	Protect plants from Allium Leaf Miner with a floating row cover. Mildew – avoid watering the leaves.		
Comments	Germination may be poor – sow seeds in groups of four to eight. Remove flower heads as soon as they appear. Harvest when they reach 5" in height.		

GROWING GUIDE: KALE			
Plant type	Annual	**Seed to harvest (in days)**	45 - 60
Frost tolerant	Yes	**Seed planting depth (inches)**	¼ inch
Zones (USDA)	2 - 10	**Sow method**	Direct sow/Indoor sow
Exposure	Full sun	**When to sow seed inside**	6 weeks before last frost
Season	Cool	**When to sow seed outdoors**	Plant from early spring to 3 months before expected fall frost date
Height (inches)	12" - 36"	**Germination time (in days)**	10 - 14
Ease-of-care	2		
Problems	Aphids – use a strong jet of water to blast them off. Protect plants from cabbage loopers & cabbage worms with a floating row cover. Watch for slugs and snails.		
Comments	Pick outside leaves as required. 'Prizm Hybrid' & 'Premier' are good varieties for a small space.		

GROWING GUIDE: LEEK			
Plant type	Biennial grown as an annual	**Seed to harvest (in days)**	80 - 110
Frost tolerant	Yes	**Seed planting depth (inches)**	½ inch
Zones (USDA)	3 - 10	**Sow method**	Direct sow/Indoor sow
Exposure	Full sun	**When to sow seed inside**	10 - 12 weeks before last frost
Season	Cool	**When to sow seed outdoors**	4 weeks before last frost
Height (inches)	15" - 30"	**Germination time (in days)**	5 - 7
Ease-of-care	3		
Problems	Protect plants from onion maggots with a floating row cover.		
Comments	Intercrop with quick-growing leafy greens. 'Lancelot' is a good variety for a small space.		

GROWING GUIDE: LETTUCE

Plant type	Annual	Seed to harvest (in days)	21 - 60
Frost tolerant	Somewhat	Seed planting depth (inches)	⅛ inch
Zones (USDA)	3 - 10	Sow method	Direct sow/indoor sow
Exposure	Full sun to partial sun	When to sow seed inside	4 weeks before last frost
Season	Cool	When to sow seed outdoors	4 weeks before last frost date
Height (inches)	6" - 12"	Germination time (in days)	7 - 14
Ease-of-care	2		
Problems	Protect plants from leaf miners, cabbage loopers and leafhoppers with a floating row cover. To prevent bolting, shade plants with row covers supported by hoops when the weather warms up. Watch for slugs.		
Comments	Thin out by cutting with scissors and use in salads. Grow lettuce for leaf cutting and also for head varieties. Choose slow-bolting varieties for planting later in the season. 'Ruby', 'Salad Bowl' & 'Bibb are good varieties for a small space.		

GROWING GUIDE: MELON			
(Cantaloupe, Honey Dew, Musk Melon)			
Plant type	Annual	**Seed to harvest (in days)**	75 - 85
Frost tolerant	No	**Seed planting depth (inches)**	½ to 1 inch
Zones (USDA)	4 - 11	**Sow method**	Direct sow/indoor sow
Exposure	Full sun	**When to sow seed inside**	4 weeks before last frost
Season	Warm	**When to sow seed outdoors**	1 – 2 weeks after last frost
Height (inches)	12" - 20"	**Germination time (in days)**	3 - 10
Ease-of-care	4		
Problems	Aphids – use a strong jet of water to blast them off. Protect plants from flea beetles, cucumber beetles and squash bugs with a floating row cover. Remove row cover at flowering time to allow pollinators access to the plant.		
Comments	Protect small seedlings from sudden cold snaps – use a one-gallon plastic milk jug with bottom removed as a temporary cover. Use a melon hammock/sling to support the fruit. 'Minnesota Midget' is a good variety for a small space.		

GROWING GUIDE: ONION			
Plant type	Biennial grown as an annual	**Seed to harvest (in days)**	-
Frost tolerant	Yes	**Seed planting depth (inches)**	1 inch
Zones (USDA)	3 - 10	**Sow method**	-
Exposure	Full sun	**When to sow seed inside**	-
Season	Cool	**When to sow seed outdoors**	Plant *'sets'* (see comment) 1" deep, 2 - 4 weeks before last frost date
Height (inches)	12" - 36"	**Germination time (in days)**	-
Ease-of-care	4		
Problems	Protect plants from onion maggot with a floating row cover.		
Comments	Grow onions from onion *sets* - immature onions. (onions grown from seed are very slow). To prevent bolting, choose sets not more than ¾ inch in diameter. 'Walla Walla', 'Superstar' & 'Red Candy Apple' are good varieties for a small space.		

GROWING GUIDE: PARSNIP

Plant type	Biennial grown as an *annual*	Seed to harvest (in days)	95 - 105
Frost tolerant	Somewhat	Seed planting depth (inches)	½ inch
Zones (USDA)	3-10	Sow method	Sow direct
Exposure	Full sun	When to sow seed inside	-
Season	Cool	When to sow seed outdoors	2 - 3 weeks before last frost date
Height (inches)	24" - 36"	Germination time (in days)	10 - 21
Ease-of-care	4		
Problems	Protect plants from carrot fly with a floating row cover.		
Comments	A vegetable that deserves to be grown more widely; lovely in a roasted vegetable medley.		

GROWING GUIDE: PEA			
Plant type	Annual - vine	**Seed to harvest (in days)**	55 - 80
Frost tolerant	Yes	**Seed planting depth (inches)**	2 inches
Zones (USDA)	Somewhat	**Sow method**	Direct sow
Exposure	Full sun	**When to sow seed inside**	-
Season	Cool	**When to sow seed outdoors**	4 weeks before last frost *in situ*
Height (inches)	2' - 8'	**Germination time (in days)**	9 - 13
Ease-of-care	2		
Problems	Aphids – use a strong jet of water to blast them off. Mildew - avoid wetting foliage.		
Comments	Transplant with care. Grow **mildew-resistant varieties**, if possible. Provide support. 'Tom Thumb', 'Peas-in-a-pot' & 'Little SnapPea Crunch' are good varieties for a small space.		

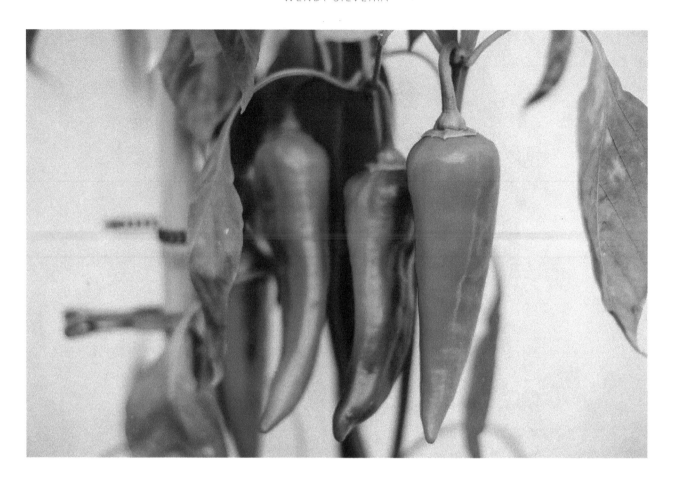

GROWING GUIDE: PEPPERS

Plant type	Annual *	Seed to harvest (in days)	50 - 80
Frost tolerant	No	Seed planting depth (inches)	¼ inch
Zones (USDA)	3 - 10	Sow method	Direct sow/indoor sow
Exposure	Full sun	When to sow seed inside	8 weeks before last frost
Season	Warm	When to sow seed outdoors	4 weeks after frost
Height (inches)	12" - 36"	Germination time (in days)	7 - 15
Ease-of-care	2 - 3		
Problems	Aphids – use a strong jet of water to blast them off. Blossom end rot.		
Comments	In some warmer areas, they may overwinter, but will often lose their vigor. Best treated as *annuals. 'Hot Paper Lantern', 'Sweet Chinese Giant', 'Thai Hot' & 'Camelot' are good varieties for a small space.		

GROWING GUIDE: POTATO

Plant type	Perennial grown as an *annual*	Seed to harvest (in days)	70 - 80
Frost tolerant	Yes	Seed planting depth (inches)	1 to 2 inches
Zones (USDA)	3 - 10	Sow method	Direct sow
Exposure	Full sun	When to sow seed inside	-
Season	Cool	When to sow seed outdoors	4 weeks before last frost *in situ*
Height (inches)	12" - 30"	Germination time (in days)	14 - 28
Ease-of-care	4		
Problems	Protect plants from beetles with a floating row cover.		
Comments	Grow potatoes in specially designed potato grow bags so that you don't have to 'hill' them. They require acid soil, so include extra peat moss in the soil mix. Grow potatoes from immature potato tubers called *'seed potatoes'*. Choose certified disease-free seed potatoes. 'All Blue', 'Red Pontiac' & 'Yukon Gold' are good varieties for a small space.		

GROWING GUIDE: RADISH			
Plant type	Annual	**Seed to harvest (in days)**	25 - 40
Frost tolerant	Yes	**Seed planting depth (inches)**	¼ inch
Zones (USDA)	2 - 10	**Sow method**	Direct sow
Exposure	Full to partial sun	**When to sow seed inside**	-
Season	Cool & warm	**When to sow seed outdoors**	4 weeks before last frost *in situ*
Height (inches)	6" - 18"	**Germination time (in days)**	6 - 10
Ease-of-care	1 - 2		
Problems	Protect plants from cabbage root maggots with a floating row cover.		
Comments	Succession sowing: Plant small quantities every two weeks up to mid-spring and then from late summer onwards. Intercrop with slower-growing crops like cabbage or squash. 'Solaris Hybrid', 'Cherry Belle' & 'Icicle' are good varieties for a small space.		

GROWING GUIDE: SPINACH			
Plant type	Annual	**Seed to harvest (in days)**	35 - 50
Frost tolerant	Somewhat	**Seed planting depth (inches)**	½ inch
Zones (USDA)	3 - 10	**Sow method**	Direct sow/indoor sow
Exposure	Full to partial sun	**When to sow seed inside**	3 – 6 weeks before last frost
Season	Cool	**When to sow seed outdoors**	4 weeks before last frost *in situ*
Height (inches)	6" - 15"	**Germination time (in days)**	6 - 10
Ease-of-care	3		
Problems	Protect plants from leaf miners with a floating row cover.		
Comments	Transplant with care. Early planting will help prevent the plant from bolting when conditions become warmer. 'Space Hybrid' is a good variety for a small space.		

GROWING GUIDE: SUMMER SQUASH (Zucchini, Courgette, Yellow Crookneck)			
Plant type	Annual	**Seed to harvest (in days)**	35 - 55
Frost tolerant	No	**Seed planting depth (inches)**	½ to 1 inch
Zones (USDA)	3 - 9	**Sow method**	Direct sow/indoor sow
Exposure	Full sun	**When to sow seed inside**	6 weeks before last frost
Season	Warm	**When to sow seed outdoors**	After all danger of frost is past
Height (inches)	12" - 36"	**Germination time (in days)**	5 - 10
Ease-of-care	2 - 3		
Problems	Protect plants from squash bugs and cucumber beetles with a floating row cover. Mildew – avoid wetting foliage.		
Comments	Does well in containers. 'Patio Green Bush', 'Golden Zebra' & 'Bush Baby' are good varieties for a small space.		

GROWING GUIDE: TOMATO

Plant type	Annual – Bush and Vine varieties	Seed to harvest (in days)	35 - 80
Frost tolerant	No	Seed planting depth (inches)	¼ inch
Zones (USDA)	3 - 10	Sow method	Direct sow/indoor sow
Exposure	Full sun	When to sow seed inside	6 weeks before last frost
Season	Warm	When to sow seed outdoors	After all danger of frost is past
Height (inches)	24" - 96"	Germination time (in days)	6 - 12
Ease-of-care	3		
Problems	Blossom end rot, mildew. Protect smaller bush varieties from squash bugs with a floating row cover, or pick off pests by hand.		
Comments	Grow **disease-resistant varieties**, if possible. Plant the tomato about 1 inch deeper than it was in the pot. Bush varieties are ideally suited to containers. Vine varieties will require support, and may be pruned to one main stem, if desired. 'Cupid', 'Tasmanian Chocolate' & 'Patio Princess' are good varieties for a small space. **For more information on cultivating tomatoes, see the front of the book.**		

GROWING GUIDE: TURNIP

Plant type	Annual	Seed to harvest (in days)	45 - 60
Frost tolerant	Yes	Seed planting depth (inches)	⅛ inch
Zones (USDA)	2 - 9	Sow method	Direct sow
Exposure	Full - partial sun	When to sow seed inside	-
Season	Cool & Warm	When to sow seed outdoors	4 weeks before last frost *in situ*
Height (inches)	6" - 12"	Germination time (in days)	4 - 10
Ease-of-care	2		
Problems	Mildew – avoid watering the leaves. Protect plants from flea beetles with a floating row cover.		
Comments	An easy-to-grow vegetable which is lovely in a roasted vegetable medley.		

GROWING GUIDE: WINTER SQUASH (Acorn, Butternut, Hubbard, Pumpkin, Spaghetti)			
Plant type	Annual	**Seed to harvest (in days)**	70 - 100
Frost tolerant	Yes	**Seed planting depth (inches)**	1 inch
Zones (USDA)	3 - 10	**Sow method**	Direct sow/Indoor sow
Exposure	Full sun	**When to sow seed inside**	2 - 4 weeks before last frost
Season	Warm	**When to sow seed outdoors**	After all danger of frost is past
Height (inches)	12" - 48"	**Germination time (in days)**	7 - 10
Ease-of-care	3 - 4		
Problems	Mildew – avoid watering the leaves		
Comments	They do take a lot of space. Grow them vertically on a strong structure and use *'hammocks'* (slings) to support the melons. Thin seedlings to **one** by cutting surplus seedlings. Protect plants from beetles with a floating row cover. Bush varieties are available, but take more space than vining varieties which can be trained up a strong support.		

GROWING GUIDE: BASIL			
Plant type	Annual	**Seed planting depth (in inches)**	¼ inch
Frost tolerant	No	**Sow method**	Direct sow preferred
Zones (USDA)	3 - 10	**When to sow seed indoors**	8 weeks before last frost
Exposure	Full sun	**When to sow seed outdoors**	2 weeks after last frost
Season	Warm	**Germination time (in days)**	5 - 15 days
Height (inches)	10" - 20"	**Problems**	Aphids – spray with a strong jet of water
Ease-of-care	2		
Comments	Do not allow it to flower – pinch out the growing tip. In very hot areas, basil will appreciate some shade. Cover with row cover to protect it from early frost.		

GROWING GUIDE: CHIVES			
Plant type	Perennial	**Seed planting depth (in inches)**	¼ inch
Frost tolerant	Yes	**Sow method**	Direct sow preferred
Zones (USDA)	3 - 9	**When to sow seed indoors**	6 – 8 weeks before last frost date
Exposure	Full sun to part sun	**When to sow seed outdoors**	4 – 6 weeks before last frost date
Season	Cool	**Germination time (in days)**	7 - 14
Height (inches)	12"	**Problems**	Aphids – spray with a strong jet of water
Ease-of-care	3		
Comments	Will go dormant in winter and come back in the spring.		

GROWING GUIDE: CILANTRO (Coriander, Chinese parsley)			
Plant type	Annual	**Seed planting depth (in inches)**	¼ inch
Frost tolerant	Somewhat	**Sow method**	Direct sow preferred
Zones (USDA)	3 - 10	**When to sow seed indoors**	6 weeks before last frost
Exposure	Full sun to partial sun	**When to sow seed outdoors**	2 weeks after last frost
Season	Cool	**Germination time (in days)**	7 - 10
Height (inches)	12" - 20"	**Problems**	Aphids – spray with a strong jet of water
Ease-of-care	2		
Comments	Will bolt in the heat. Remove flower heads as they appear to prevent seed production. Use row cover to protect the plant from frost.		

GROWING GUIDE: DILL

Plant type	Annual	Seed planting depth (in inches)	¼ inch
Frost tolerant	No	Sow method	Direct sow preferred
Zones (USDA)	2 - 11	When to sow seed indoors	6 weeks before last frost
Exposure	Full sun	When to sow seed outdoors	2 weeks after last frost *in situ*
Season	Cool	Germination time (in days)	7 - 21
Height (inches)	36"	Problems	Aphids–spray with a strong jet of water
Ease-of-care	2		
Comments	Transplant with care. Will bolt in the heat. Remove flower heads as they appear to prevent seed production.		

GROWING GUIDE: LAVENDER			
Plant type	Perennial shrub*	**Seed planting depth (in inches)**	-
Frost tolerant	Somewhat	**Sow method**	-
Zones (USDA)	5 - 9	**When to sow seed indoors**	-
Exposure	Full sun	**When to sow seed outdoors**	-
Season	Warm	**Germination time (in days)**	-
Height (inches)	18" - 30"	**Problems**	-
Ease-of-care	2		
Comments	*Buy potted plants. Needs good drainage. Will go dormant in cold winters and come back in the spring. Highly suited to growing in a container. Good cut flower and dries well too. Cut back after flowering.		

GROWING GUIDE: OREGANO

Plant type	Perennial	Seed planting depth (in inches)	Cover very lightly
Frost tolerant	Somewhat	Sow method	Indoor sow preferred
Zones (USDA)	5 - 10	When to sow seed indoors	8 weeks before last frost
Exposure	Full sun	When to sow seed outdoors	2 weeks after last frost
Season	Warm	Germination time (in days)	4 - 8
Height (inches)	8" - 16"	Problems	-
Ease-of-care	1		
Comments	May even be hardy in sheltered spots in zone 4. Oregano can be dried very easily.		

GROWING GUIDE: PARSLEY			
Plant type	Annual	**Seed planting depth (in inches)**	¼ inch
Frost tolerant	Yes	**Sow method**	Sow direct/indoor sow
Zones (USDA)	5a - 9b	**When to sow seed indoors**	8 weeks before last frost
Exposure	Full to partial sun	**When to sow seed outdoors**	2 weeks after last frost
Season	Cool	**Germination time (in days)**	21 - 28
Height (inches)	18" - 20"	**Problems**	-
Ease-of-care	2		
Comments	In hot regions, parsley will appreciate some afternoon shade, as it dries very easily.		

GROWING GUIDE: ROSEMARY			
Plant type	Perennial shrub*	**Seed planting depth (in inches)**	-
Frost tolerant	Somewhat	**Sow method**	-
Zones (USDA)	9 - 11	**When to sow seed indoors**	-
Exposure	Full sun	**When to sow seed outdoors**	-
Season	Warm	**Germination time (in days)**	-
Height (inches)	24" - 36"	**Problems**	-
Ease-of-care	1		
Comments	*Purchase nursery-grown plants. Needs good drainage. Will go dormant in cold winters and come back in the spring. Highly suited to growing in a container.		

GROWING GUIDE: SAGE			
Plant type	Perennial	**Seed planting depth (in inches)**	¼ inch
Frost tolerant	Yes	**Sow method**	Sow direct/indoor sow
Zones (USDA)	5 - 9	**When to sow seed indoors**	6 weeks before last frost
Exposure	Full sun	**When to sow seed outdoors**	2 weeks after last frost
Season	Cool	**Germination time (in days)**	6 - 10
Height (inches)	12" - 18"	**Problems**	-
Ease-of-care	2		
Comments	Will go dormant in cold winters and come back in the spring. Harvest this perennial sparingly the first year.		

GROWING GUIDE: THYME			
Plant type	Perennial	**Seed planting depth (in inches)**	⅛ inch
Frost tolerant	Somewhat	**Sow method**	Direct sow/Indoor sow preferred
Zones (USDA)	5 - 9	**When to sow seed indoors**	6 weeks before last frost
Exposure	Full sun	**When to sow seed outdoors**	2 weeks after last frost
Season	Cool	**Germination time (in days)**	3 - 7
Height (inches)	8" - 12"	**Problems**	-
Ease-of-care	1		
Comments	Will go dormant in winter and come back in the spring. Grow an assortment of thymes: Lemon, English, French.		

GROWING GUIDE: APPLE			
Plant type	Deciduous perennial	**Variety**	Choose a variety suitable for your area.
Frost tolerant	Yes, but harvest before frost	**Suitable for a container**	Yes
Zones (USDA)	5 - 9	**Self-pollinating**	May require a second tree to cross-pollinate
Exposure	Full sun		
Comments	Check that the apple is grafted onto a rootstock labeled *'dwarf rootstock'*. Choose a large container: A one-year-old apple tree will need a 15-gallon pot. Add extra drainage holes. When planting, ensure that the 'graft union' is above the level of the soil. Mulch the tree with 2" of organic material.		

GROWING GUIDE: BLUEBERRY			
Plant type	Fruit	**Variety**	Choose a variety suitable for your zone
Frost tolerant	Yes* but differs by variety	**Suitable for a container**	Yes
Zones (USDA)	3 - 9	**Self-pollinating**	Check on the plant label
Exposure	Full sun		
Problems	Damage to the fruit by birds. Protect with netting preferably draped over a frame.		
Comments	*Cover if severe frost is expected. Select a self-pollinating variety, or plant two blueberries to ensure pollination. Blueberries require a *strongly acidic soil* of **4.8 to 5.0**. Include peat moss at planting. Mulch the bush with 2" of organic material. Feed with an acidic fertilizer suitable for Azaleas *only at bloom time*.		

GROWING GUIDE: LEMON

Plant type	Evergreen perennial	Variety	Dwarf 'Meyer' lemon on dwarf rootstock
Frost tolerant	No	**Suitable for a container**	Yes
Zones (USDA)	9 – 11* (move indoors in winter)	**Self-pollinating**	Yes
Exposure	Full sun	**Pruning**	Damaged wood or crossed stems
Height (inches)			
Problems	Use a soap spray for scale insects or mealybugs.		
Comments	Check that the lemon is grafted onto a rootstock labeled *'dwarf rootstock.'* When planting, ensure that the 'graft union' is above the level of the soil. *In zones 8 and below, put the container on a plant caddy so that it can be moved indoors. Position in front of a sunny window. Lemons do not like 'wet feet'. Use a 'cactus mix potting soil' to ensure quick drainage. Add a few extra drainage holes to the container. Don't overwater. Fertilize with an organic slow-release fertilizer specially formulated for citrus in early spring, mid-summer and early fall. Mulch with a 2" layer of organic materials. Keep mulch away from the trunk of the lemon tree.		

GROWING GUIDE: STRAWBERRY			
Plant type	Fruit	**Variety**	Choose varieties suitable for your area
Frost tolerant	Somewhat but provide protection	**Suitable for a container**	Yes
Zones (USDA)	3 - 10	**Self-pollinating**	-
Exposure	Full sun*		
Problems	Damage to the fruit by birds. Protect with netting preferably draped over a frame.		
Comments	*In southern areas, plants will benefit from shade later in the day. When planting, ensure that the *central growing crown is above the soil level*. Avoid watering the leaves. Mulch the bush with 2" of organic material. Feed regularly with fertilizer for fruit trees, beginning one month after planting. In the first year, pinch off the flowers to enable the plant to establish a strong root system. Use row cover to protect strawberries from severe frost, and netting to prevent bird attacks. Strawberries will multiply by runners. Only cultivate the *first* runner.		

GROWING GUIDE: ACHILLEA (Yarrow)

Plant type	Perennial	Seed planting depth (inches)	Do not cover seed
Zones (USDA)	5 - 8	Sow method	Direct Sow / Indoor Sow
Exposure	Full sun	When to sow seed indoors	8 - 10 weeks before last frost
Bloom season	Spring and summer	When to sow seed outdoors	Sow in late spring or fall
Height (inches)	20" - 30"	Germination time (in days)	10 - 14
Ease-of-care	2	Bloom color	White, pink, yellow, rose red.
Problems		Attracts	Pollinators, birds and ladybugs
Comments	Good long-lasting, 'filler' plant for flower arrangements. Can also be dried. Highly suited to containers where growth can be contained. Deadhead to extend the flowering season.		

GROWING GUIDE: ALSTROEMERIA
(Inca Lily, Peruvian lily)

Plant type	Perennial	**Seed planting depth (inches)**	-
Zones (USDA)	8 - 10*	**Sow method**	-
Exposure	Full sun	**When to sow seed indoors**	-
Bloom season	Spring, summer & fall	**When to sow seed outdoors**	-
Height (inches)	12" - 36"	**Germination time (in days)**	-
Ease-of-care	2	**Bloom color**	White, yellow, orange, pink, red, mauve, purple
Problems	Aphids – blast with a jet of water	**Attracts**	Pollinators
Comments	*Will need protection during winter in zone 7 and below. Purchase potted plants. *Superb florist-quality cut* flower which will last 10 – 14 days in the vase. Does very well in a large container.		

GROWING GUIDE: COSMOS

Plant type	Annual	**Seed planting depth (inches)**	¼ inch
Zones (USDA)	All	**Sow method**	Direct sow/indoor sow
Exposure	Full sun	**When to sow seed indoors**	Plant indoors 2 – 3 weeks before the last freeze
Bloom season	Summer/Early fall	**When to sow seed outdoors**	After the last frost
Height (inches)	15"- 48"	**Germination time (in days)**	7 - 10
Ease-of-care	1	**Bloom color**	White, pink, red,
Problems	Aphids – blast with a jet of water	**Attracts**	Birds, bees and beneficial insects
Comments	Good cut flower. Deadhead to lengthen the blooming season. Does well in a container.		

GROWING GUIDE: DAHLIA

Plant type	Perennial tuber	Seed planting depth (inches)	-
Zones (USDA)	2 - 11	Sow method	-
Exposure	Full sun	When to sow seed indoors	-
Bloom season	Midsummer through fall	When to sow seed outdoors	-
Height (inches)	30" - 120"	Germination time (in days)	-
Ease-of-care	3 - 4	Bloom color	All colors
Problems	Watch for slugs and snails	Attracts	Bees
Comments	Excellent, showy cut flower grown from tubers (bulbs) Will need support with 1- 2 tall stakes per plant. In the fall, before the ground freezes, and after the plants have died back, cut stems down to 2-4" above the soil line. Carefully dig tubers and remove excess soil. Store them in a warm, dark place, like a garage, over winter. Replant in late spring. In zones 8 and above you may leave tubers in the ground over winter. Does well in a large container.		

GROWING GUIDE: FREESIA

Plant type	Perennial bulb	Seed planting depth (inches)	-
Zones (USDA)	3 - 9*	Sow method	-
Exposure	Full sun to light shade	When to sow seed indoors	-
Bloom season	Early spring	When to sow seed outdoors	-
Height (inches)	12" - 18"	Germination time (in days)	-
Ease-of-care	2	Bloom color	White, yellow, pink mauve, red
Problems	Aphids – blast with a jet of water	Attracts	Pollinators and birds
Comments	*In zones 8 and below freesias, which are grown from bulbs, will not survive the winter outdoors; treat them as annuals. Freesias have intense fragrance and make great cut flowers. They are ideally suited to growing in a deep container.		

GROWING GUIDE: LILY

Plant type	Perennial bulb	Seed planting depth (inches)	-
Zones (USDA)	3 - 9	Sow method	-
Exposure	Full – partial sun	When to sow seed indoors	-
Bloom season	Late spring - summer	When to sow seed outdoors	-
Height (inches)	12" - 84"	Germination time (in days)	-
Ease-of-care	2	Bloom color	All colors
Problems	Aphids – blast with a jet of water. Treat lily leaf beetles with Neem oil.	Attracts	Butterflies and hummingbirds
Comments	Plant bulbs in fall and spring for spectacular blooms. Taller varieties may require staking. Cut flowers when the buds are showing color and have swelled, but not yet open. When cutting, don't remove more than ⅓ of the stem. Some varieties are very fragrant Leave bulbs to overwinter in the ground. Over time they will multiply. Does well in a large container.		

GROWING GUIDE: MARIGOLD			
Plant type	Annual	**Seed planting depth (inches)**	¼ inch
Zones (USDA)	All	**Sow method**	Direct Sow/Indoor Sow
Exposure	Full sun	**When to sow seed indoors**	4-6 weeks before the last frost
Bloom season	Spring, summer, fall	**When to sow seed outdoors**	After all danger of frost is past
Height (inches)	6" - 40"	**Germination time (in days)**	7 - 14
Ease-of-care	1	**Bloom color**	Cream, yellow, orange, maroon
Problems	Aphids – use a strong jet of water to blast them off.	**Attracts**	Beneficial insects, birds bees and butterflies
Comments	Interplant among vegetables to prevent pests and disease, or grow in a container. Taller varieties are suitable for cutting. Deadhead to extend the flowering season.		

GROWING GUIDE: PEONY			
Plant type	Perennial root	**Seed planting depth (inches)**	-
Zones (USDA)	3 - 8*	**Sow method**	-
Exposure	Full sun	**When to sow seed indoors**	-
Bloom season	Spring - early summer	**When to sow seed outdoors**	-
Height (inches)	15" - 36"	**Germination time (in days)**	-
Ease-of-care	3 - 4	**Bloom color**	White, pink, red, maroon, yellow
Problems		**Attracts**	Ants – ignore them
Comments	* May grow in zone 9 in cooler micro-climate spots - choose *early-flowering* varieties. Peonies are propagated by division of roots. Grow them in a large container; they don't like their roots being disturbed. You may have to stake the flowering stems of some varieties. Deadhead to extend the flowering season. Some varieties are very fragrant. Exceptional cut flowers.		

GROWING GUIDE: ROSE			
Plant type	Perennial	**Seed planting depth (inches)**	-
Zones (USDA)	4 - 11*	**Sow method**	-
Exposure	Full sun	**When to sow seed indoors**	-
Bloom season	Spring, summer, fall	**When to sow seed outdoors**	-
Height (inches)	12" - 48"'	**Germination time (in days)**	-
Ease-of-care	3 - 4	**Bloom color**	White, peach, pink, yellow, orange, red, mauve, purple
Problems	Aphids, spider mites, mildew and black spot	**Attracts**	Hummingbirds, butterflies, bees
Comments	*Select a variety suitable for your zone. Roses need a very large container. Choose a variety that is labeled *disease-resistant*. Roses come in a wide variety of forms - hybrid-tea roses are single-stemmed; floribundas flower in a truss (group) of smaller flowers. Deadhead to extend the flowering season. Prune in winter. Fragrance differs by variety. If possible, buy ready-potted roses rather than bare-root stock roses.		

GROWING GUIDE: SWEET PEA

Plant type	Annual vine and bush varieties	**Seed planting depth (inches)**	2"
Zones (USDA)	2 - 11	**Sow method**	Direct sow
Exposure	Full sun	**When to sow seed indoors**	4-5 weeks before the last frost
Bloom season	Spring – early summer	**When to sow seed outdoors**	Late fall to early spring
Height (inches)	12" - 60"	**Germination time (in days)**	10 - 14
Ease-of-care	3	**Bloom color**	White, Blue, Pink, Lavender, Red
Problems	Aphids, caterpillars, slugs and snails	**Attracts**	Butterflies, bees and bumblebees
Comments	Soak the seed in warm (not boiling) water for up to 24 hours before sowing. Non-bush varieties will require support with sweet pea netting or tall trellis. Deadhead to extend the flowering season. Sweet peas perform best in cool weather and are prized for their fragrance. Does well in a large container.		

GROWING GUIDE: ZINNIA			
Plant type	Annual	**Seed planting depth (inches)**	¼ inch
Zones (USDA)	All	**Sow method**	Direct Sow/Indoor Sow
Exposure	Full sun	**When to sow seed indoors**	Sow 4 weeks before last frost
Bloom season	Summer	**When to sow seed outdoors**	After last frost
Height (inches)	12" - 30"	**Germination time (in days)**	7 - 10
Ease-of-care	1	**Bloom color**	White, yellow, pink, purple, red
Problems	Mildew – avoid wetting the foliage	**Attracts**	Beneficial insects
Comments	Cut stems before the flowers are fully open. They are great pollinators and are a magnet for hummingbirds and butterflies. Deadhead to extend the flowering season. Does well in a large container.		

Chapter 7

Tried And Tested Recipes

From Your Garden To Your Table

Gardening is cheaper than therapy and you get tomatoes.
~Author Unknown

This chapter presents a few of my favorite recipes that my family and friends have enjoyed for many years.

All these recipes include ingredients that I have grown in my garden.

There is a simple pleasure in being able to harvest from your garden and make it into something delicious for your table.

Always try to grow your herbs as close to the kitchen as possible. That's why it is called a kitchen garden!

APPLESAUCE MUFFINS

For Muffins
1 ½ cups all purpose (plain) flour
1 ½ tsp baking powder
½ tsp baking soda
½ tsp cinnamon
½ tsp allspice
¼ tsp grated nutmeg
¼ tsp salt
2 large eggs
1 cup brown sugar (packed)
1 stick (½ cup, 4oz, 115g), plus 3 tablespoons of unsalted butter, melted (total: 5.5oz)
1 cup applesauce (recipe follows)
I cup (3 ½ oz) pecans or walnuts, coarsely chopped

For Topping
2 TBL granulated sugar
¼ tsp cinnamon
¼ tsp allspice
¼ tsp grated nutmeg
Stir all topping ingredients together and set aside.

Instructions
Preheat oven to 400F°.
Grease 6-hole Jumbo (Texas-style) (250ml/8oz capacity) muffin pan.
Stir together flour, baking powder, baking soda, spices, and salt in a bowl.
In an electric mixer, beat eggs and brown sugar for a couple of minutes. Then add butter, a little at a time, beating until mixture is creamy. Stir in applesauce, then fold in flour until all flour is absorbed, but don't overmix. Stir in nuts and divide batter among the muffin cups. Sprinkle topping on top of muffins. Bake for 25 minutes or until a skewer comes out clean. Leave in pan for 5 minutes. Cool on a cooling rack.

Makes 6 large (jumbo) muffins

APPLESAUCE

Ingredients

3 pounds of apples, peeled, cored and cut into rough ¾ inch pieces

1 cup water

1/3 cup brown sugar (packed)

2 TBL fresh lemon juice

½ tsp cinnamon

Instructions

Combine apples, water and brown sugar in a medium saucepan.

Bring to a boil, stirring occasionally. Reduce heat, cover and simmer until apples are fork-tender, about 25 minutes. Uncover and simmer until almost all liquid has evaporated, about 5 -7 minutes. Remove from heat. Stir in lemon juice and cinnamon. Cool for about 30 minutes. With a potato masher or fork, mash apple mixture until coarse and chunky. Keeps in the refrigerator for 3 days. Freezes well. (I freeze it in 1 cup batches for use in the applesauce muffin recipe.)

Makes about 3 cups

BLUEBERRY MUFFINS

Ingredients
2 ⅓ cups self-rising flour
½ cup all purpose (plain) flour
½ cup plus 2 TBL soft brown sugar
1 cup fresh or frozen blueberries
2 eggs
1 cup milk
1 tsp vanilla extract
1 stick (½ cup, 4oz, 115g) unsalted butter, melted
Powdered (Icing) sugar, to dust

Instructions
Preheat the oven to hot 415F°.
Grease a 6-hole Jumbo (Texas-style) (250ml/8oz capacity) muffin tin with melted butter. Sift the flours into a large mixing bowl. Stir in the sugar and blueberries, and make a well in the center. With a fork, whisk the eggs, milk and vanilla together, and add to the well in the dry ingredients. Add the butter, and stir until just combined. Do not overmix. Spoon the mixture evenly into the muffin tin, filling each hole about ¾ full. Bake for 23 – 25 minutes, or until a skewer comes out clean. Leave the muffins in the pan for 5 minutes. Cool on a wire rack. Dust generously with powdered sugar just before serving.

Makes 6 large (jumbo) muffins

COUSCOUS SALAD WITH HERBS AND FETA CHEESE

Ingredients

3 cups prepared couscous, or 1 pre-packaged box instant couscous (about 5 oz)

½ tsp black pepper

2 TBL lemon juice

3 TBL olive oil

2 large firm tomatoes, chopped (Roma work well) into half-inch pieces

1 medium zucchini, halved and thinly sliced

½ cup fresh basil, cut into strips

1/3 cup green (spring) onions, sliced

1 cup crumbled feta cheese, preferably herb-flavored

Instructions

Prepare couscous according to directions: Add black pepper to the water, but omit butter or olive oil. In a large bowl, combine prepared couscous, lemon juice and olive oil. Then add tomatoes, zucchini, basil, green onions and feta cheese. Mix gently. Cover and chill for 4 - 6 hours or overnight.

JEAN'S ZUCCHINI BREAD

Ingredients

3 eggs

1 cup vegetable oil

2 cups granulated sugar

2 tsp vanilla

2 cups grated zucchini

3 cups all purpose (plain) flour

1 tsp baking soda

¼ tsp baking powder

3 tsp cinnamon

1 tsp salt

½ cup walnuts or pecans

Instructions

Preheat the oven to 325F°.
Beat eggs, then add oil,
sugar and vanilla together
for a couple of minutes.

Add zucchini and mix gently. Sift flour, baking soda, baking powder, cinnamon and salt. Add the flour mixture to the wet mixture until just blended. Then add nuts. Divide mixture between two greased 9" X 5" loaf pans. Bake for about 1 hour. A skewer should come out clean. Place pans on cooling rack for 5 minutes and then turn out and leave to cool on cooling rack.

(makes 2 loaves – freezes well)

LEMON MADEIRA LOAF

Ingredients
6 TBL (3oz) butter
1 cup white sugar
1½ cups sifted all purpose (plain) flour
Slightly less than ½ cup milk
Pinch of salt
2 eggs, beaten
1 large lemon (or 2 small lemons) – for zesting and juice
2 tsp baking powder

Instructions
Preheat oven to 350F°.

Grease a 9" x 5" loaf pan, and line with parchment paper or butter papers. Grease paper lightly. Zest the entire washed lemon. Cream butter and sugar until light and fluffy. Add well beaten eggs and grated zest (lemon rind) Mix dry ingredients together. Stir into creamed butter mixture, alternatively with milk.

Bake for about 45 minutes, or until a skewer comes out clean. While the cake is in the oven, make the **syrup** of ½ cup of sugar and juice of the lemon. This will dissolve while the cake is baking. Remove the cake from oven and while still hot, pour syrup over it. When all soaked in, remove from pan onto wire rack. Remove butter papers and leave on rack to cool.

Makes one loaf

SPAGHETTI BOLOGNESE SAUCE

Ingredients

2 TBL olive oil

2 medium onions, finely chopped

4 cloves of garlic, crushed

1 lb. (500g) minced beef

2 x 14.5 oz (411g) cans tomatoes (one Italian stewed, one Italian diced)

3 oz (85g) or ½ can tomato paste

1 x 8 oz (227g) can tomato sauce

1 tsp dried oregano

1 tsp dried parsley

1 tsp dried basil

½ tsp dried marjoram

3 tsp beef stock powder

1 tsp brown sugar

½ cup (125ml) dry red wine

Black pepper and sea salt to taste

8 oz (227g) mushrooms, halved (or quartered if they are large)

Handful of fresh herbs combined– oregano, parsley and marjoram (Leave whole)

¼ cup shredded fresh basil

Instructions

Heat oil in a large pan. Add onions and garlic, cook, stirring, until onions are very soft. Add mince, cook, stirring, until it changes in color. Stir in undrained tomatoes, paste, sauce, dried herbs, stock powder, brown sugar, wine, pepper and salt. Bring to the boil, reduce heat to low and add mushrooms and fresh herbs. Cover and simmer gently about 2 hours, stirring occasionally. Remove herb stems and stir in shredded basil. Serve with pasta of your choice and Parmesan cheese.

Serves 6. Make about 5 cups (1.25 liters)

SPINACH SALAD WITH HONEY DRESSING

Ingredients
Dressing
2 TBL honey
2 TBL white wine vinegar
1 TBL water
1 tsp vegetable or olive oil
¼ tsp ground black pepper
¼ tsp nutmeg

Salad
½ lb. fresh baby spinach leaves
1 can (11 oz, 312 g) mandarin
oranges, drained
1 cup fresh strawberries, halved

Instructions
Combine dressing ingredients in a
jug or small bowl, then mix well.
Drain juice from mandarin
oranges. Halve strawberries.
Arrange spinach in a large bowl,
top with oranges and strawberries
Pour dressing over top and toss to
coat.

The Gardening Journey Continues

Old gardeners never die, they just run out of thyme.
~ Gardening Saying

If you've followed the gardening techniques and strategies that I've shared with you, then I'm confident that you are reaping the benefits from whatever space is available to you.

Whether you are into containers or raised beds or both, your garden can supply you with vegetables, herbs, fruit and cut flowers throughout the year.

I hope I have awakened the spirit of gardening within you, and that you have discovered the joy that gardening brings to so many.

As you continue on your gardening journey, I invite you to visit my website. All of the gardening products discussed in the book are available at **wendysgardenstore.com/store**. This diverse range of products will help you become more successful in your garden. Become a member of my website to continue your gardening journey.

International Hardiness Zones

Australia:

http://www.anbg.gov.au/gardens/research/hort.research/zones.html

Canada:

http://www.planthardiness.gc.ca/?m=1

Europe (By country):

http://www.bc-naklo.si/fileadmin/Vertikalne_ozelenitve_pdf/Ang_3_poglavje/3.1.1.pdf

South Africa:

https://www.plantmaps.com/interactive-south-africa-plant-hardiness-zone-map-celsius.ph

Index